KITESURFING

John Wiley & Sons, Ltd

KRISTIN BOESE AND CHRISTIAN SPRECKELS

KITESURFING

THE COMPLETE GUIDE

**Translated by
Julie Roberts**

John Wiley & Sons, Ltd

WILEY NAUTICAL

Copyright © Verlag pietsch , Postfach 103742, 70032 Stuttgart.
A company of Paul Pietsch-Verlage GmbH & Co.
ISBN 978-3-613-50533-9 German Edition
1st Edition 2007

Translation © 2008 John Wiley & Sons Ltd, The Atrium, Southern Gate, Chichester, West Sussex PO19 8SQ, England
            Telephone (+44) 1243 779777

Email (for orders and customer service enquiries): cs-books@wiley.co.uk
Visit our Home Page on www.wiley.com

Other Wiley Editorial Offices

John Wiley & Sons Inc., 111 River Street, Hoboken, NJ 07030, USA

Jossey-Bass, 989 Market Street, San Francisco, CA 94103-1741, USA

Wiley-VCH Verlag GmbH, Boschstr. 12, D-69469 Weinheim, Germany

John Wiley & Sons Australia Ltd, 42 McDougall Street, Milton, Queensland 4064, Australia

John Wiley & Sons (Asia) Pte Ltd, 2 Clementi Loop #02-01, Jin Xing Distripark, Singapore 129809

John Wiley & Sons Canada Ltd, 6045 Freemont Blvd. Mississauga, Ontario, L5R 4J3 Canada

Wiley also publishes its books in a variety of electronic formats. Some content that appears in print may not be available in electronic books.

Library of Congress Cataloging-in-Publication Data

  Spreckels, Christian.
  Kitesurfing with Kristin Boese / Christian Spreckels ; translated by Julie Roberts. — 1st ed.
     p. cm.
  "The world champion's training program."
  Includes bibliographical references.
  ISBN 978-0-470-72791-1
  1. Kite surfing. 2. Boese, Kristin, 1977- I. Title.
  GV840.K49.S67 2007
  797.3—dc22

                                                2007050335

British Library Cataloguing in Publication Data
A catalogue record for this book is available from the British Library

ISBN: 978-0-470-72791-1 (PB)

Cover design: Simon Goggin

Typeset by Stephen Dent, Bath
Printed and bound in Italy by Printer Trento, Trento

This book is printed on acid-free paper responsibly manufactured from sustainable forestry
in which at least two trees are planted for each one used for paper production.

Contents

Introduction

Surfing is the sport of kings. Although riding the billowing waves was practised by members of all social classes long ago in Oceania, the kings enjoyed the privilege of using special surf boards and of being able to surf on beaches that were closed to commoners. We don't wish to enter into competition with surfing, especially since the oldest type of water sport and the newest complement one another so marvellously. But it's worth asking here what the wave-riding royalty of Oceania would have felt if in addition to their sport, which was also an integral part of their culture, they had discovered the enjoyment to be derived from kitesurfing: because kitesurfing is the sport that combines the elements. The boundary between water and air dissolves in a fluid transition: for seconds at a time the kitesurfer is aloft, floating above the water on his kite and experiencing a sense of virtual 'zero gravity' before landing on the ocean again, only to take off once more after brief contact with the water. Or he rides the wave on his small board, so that time seems to stand still. A feeling of being at one with

oneself and with nature is produced; boundaries melt away. It is this feeling that drives kitesurfers and other extreme sports athletes out onto the ocean time and again and gets them hooked; they love the sea, the sky so close above them, and the wind, which bestows power, propulsion and perhaps even something a little regal.

This deeply satisfying sensation is not just reserved for the experts, however. Even learners can experience it – for the first metres travelled, however many they may be, offer a glimpse of how wonderful it is to practise this sport and of how many unforgettable moments it holds in store. This book shows possible ways of achieving this.

The learning process is underpinned by an exercise and training programme geared to the latest theories in movement research and training theory. Basic training tips are given that enable you to learn quickly and above all safely how to kitesurf. To this end, both training and preparation measures ashore and mental imaging (or training) are introduced to complement the programme. To produce

the movement and action imagery required for this, precise descriptions are given of individual tricks, and self-instructions are suggested for the key phases. Furthermore, we detail both active and passive safety measures and recommendations for training in your kite-free time. These include using the related sports of snowboarding or wakeboarding and targeted strengthening of the muscles.

This training programme is not intended to take the place of beginners' lessons at a kitesurfing school – which we strongly recommend! Instead the programme builds on the contents of a beginners' training course, and we give you brief reminders of these contents. Depending on your level of skill and individual requirements, and what you want to achieve, the book will help you to learn more quickly and easily how to kitesurf, or how to extend and optimize your existing skills.

We wish you success, and above all lots of fun on the water!

Kristin Boese and *Christian Spreckels*

BEFORE

In this first part we list what's important for carrying out a training unit successfully on the water and why. 'Successful' in this context means that your time on the water is accident- and injury-free and also that you achieve exactly what should have been achieved at the end of the training unit: fun and successful tricks and/or surfing.

1 Safety first

008

Let's be honest, in all types of extreme sports, a bit of risk concentrates the mind and thus ensures the celebrated *flow* experience (see Chapter 2.1). This risk is a constant companion of nearly all extreme sports and so is present to a greater or lesser degree in kitesurfing, depending on one's attitude and ability. However, this statement shouldn't be misunderstood: the risk arising can and should be carefully regulated, because on the one hand we naturally wish to avoid risks or render them manageable, and on the other hand because risks can trigger anxiety. And anxiety obstructs advances in learning as well as obstructing the *flow* experience. The characteristic of a person in *flow* that we should aim for is that the person is in control of his actions and of the environment, an aim that is essential in kiting and which prevents injury. A residual risk exists nevertheless, often due to an overestimation of one's own abilities or to underestimating the

external conditions. This can lead to minor, or even severe, injuries.

A large-scale survey by W Petersen *et al.* (2002; see Bibliography) of injuries in kitesurfing showed that seven injuries occur per 1000 hours of activity. Looked at from a purely statistical perspective, this means that if 50 kitesurfers are kiting in a particular spot, one of them is injured every three hours. This quota elevates kitesurfing to an extreme sport. (However, it should be noted that this survey was undertaken before the 5-liner came onto the market. 5-liners seem to cut the injury rate, but as yet no surveys have been carried out.) The 'top 4' injuries with their percentages are:

28% foot;
14% head;
13% ribs;
13% knee.

These figures underline the need to take active and passive safety precautions.

Active safety precautions

Unfortunately, kitesurfing repeatedly gives rise to hazardous situations and to injuries that could be avoided by taking active safety measures. The recommended safety precautions are:

■ **Use constant wind conditions where possible!** The first of the recommended active safety precautions is suggested in a study on possible injuries in kitesurfing by Ziegler *et al.* (2005; see Bibliography). This study shows that 'in regions in which constant wind conditions (for example, thermal winds or trade winds) prevailed all year round, the accident rate was significantly lower than the accident rate in regions with changing winds'. Many kitesurfers answer the question as to when they should go kiting by looking at the 'wind pages' on the Internet. These may forecast the expected wind conditions relatively accurately, but provide insufficient or no information

KITING

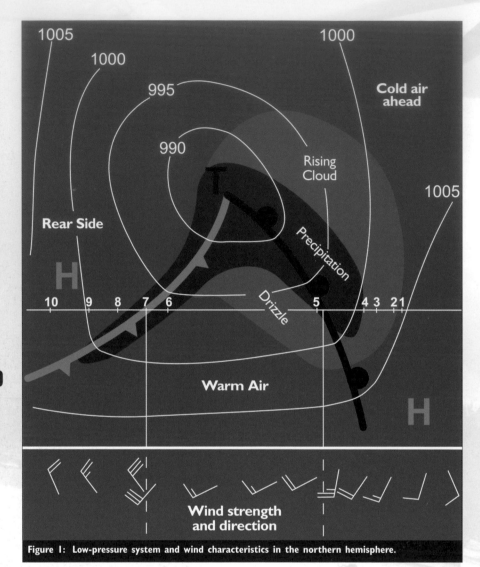

1005
1000
995
990

Cold air ahead

Rising Cloud

Precipitation

T

Rear Side

Drizzle

1005

H

10 9 8 7 6   5   4 3 2 1

Warm Air

H

Wind strength and direction

Figure 1: Low-pressure system and wind characteristics in the northern hemisphere.

010

about the corresponding meteorological conditions and weather fronts. And in the low-pressure systems triggered by the jet stream, there's a danger of rapid changes in the weather and above all of a change in the wind conditions, both with regard to direction and strength.

In a low-pressure system, a warm front precedes a cold front. Until the faster-moving cold air has overtaken the slower warm air, there are often days on which rotation around the

core of the low pressure increases, and with it, the wind speed. In and ahead of warm fronts, which are heralded by layered rain clouds and in which the prevailing wind direction is south-west, the weather is often very squally. Strong, showery gusts frequently cause dramatic variations in the wind strength in a matter of seconds. In the warm sector, there's a temporary calm in the weather and the squally conditions abate until the cold front arrives. With a cold front, the approaching

cold air pushes under the warm air, forcing the latter up over it – this type of front is recognizable by dark, vertical cloud formations – and heavy rain follows, accompanied by changeable, strong winds. Thunderstorms may also occur. Anyone going kiting in these wind conditions is naturally in danger of losing control of the kite, which is a very frequent cause of accidents. We therefore recommend that you pay heed not only to the wind strength, but also to the related frontal system. If possible let the front pass in order that you can then use the rear of the frontal system for kiting; we advise caution once the front has passed because the heavy showers and storms may persist, although generally the wind decreases in strength and is more constant. The sun also reappears once the front has passed – an essential element for a good day's kiting. Of course, our typical **high-pressure conditions** also bring a lot of sun. This isn't the only factor that makes such conditions ideal for kitesurfing: in high-pressure systems there are no fronts, in the northern hemisphere the wind blows from an easterly direction, is thermally strengthened as the land masses heat up and is normally very constant. Unfortunately, in our latitudes (especially north of Germany) these weather conditions virtually only occur in summer, especially in May and June.

Many local wind systems occur around the globe, a number of which offer extremely constant wind conditions that are sometimes well suited to kitesurfing. In most cases these conditions are dependent on the time of year and are dictated by temperature. A couple of examples are the famous *Freemantle Doctor* in **Western Australia**, which blows from October to February, giving good kitesurfing conditions: the sea breeze occurs as a result of the land masses in the great Australian desert heating up, giving rise to a thermal low-pressure area that reaches maximum effect in the afternoon. The *Cape Doctor*, which blows in and around Cape Town in **South Africa**, is a similar phenomenon and can also be very strong. But this problem can be countered by travelling west along the coast, where the wind is somewhat weaker for the most part. The south-east trade wind prevailing in the southern hemisphere provides settled kiting weather on the coast of **Brazil** from October to November. The **Canary Islands** also offer good conditions in the summer months from April to roughly the end of September thanks to the prevailing north-east trade wind, which moves further south in the winter months and can be picked up on the **Cape Verde Islands**. In the **eastern Mediterranean,** the Etesian winds provide constant kiting conditions from April to September. **Tarifa** has advertised itself for years with the slogan 'Wind capital – 365 windy days', although this is naturally a somewhat exaggerated claim. In summer, when the southerly edge of an Azores high and the northerly edge of a thermal low over Africa meet, the Levanter occurs to a greater extent here. This wind, which is accelerated by the Straits of Gibraltar, is sometimes extremely strong and very gusty, and around Tarifa it also blows offshore, so that the Poniente, which is considerably weaker but more consistent and blows from the south-west, is far more popular with kitesurfers. Unfortunately, it's often too weak. Opposite Tarifa, the coast of **Morocco** stretches for over 2500 kilometres. This coast boasts many beaches with wind and waves for kitesurfing. The north-east trade wind drives local, thermal wind systems here too during the summer months. Here the wind can also become very strong and blow hard for several weeks. The wind in **Guincho** on the west coast of **Portugal** is similarly strong. As in **Sagres** on the western edge of the

Iberian heat low (a low-pressure system caused by heat), the northerly winds here in Guincho are strengthened by local thermals. We could continue with this list indefinitely, but we'll stop at this point, because the quest to find a suitable location is just as much a part of kitesurfing as waiting patiently for the wind, which, hopefully, will then blow constantly.

■ **Choice of location:** The choice of a suitable kiting location is dictated not only by conditions on the water, but also by aspects on shore that are worth noting. Depending on the wind direction, consideration should always be given as to whether a good opportunity exists for launching and landing the kite, and if so – where. Kitesurfers must always be able to answer the question, 'Can passers-by or bathers be put in danger?' with a 'No'.

The decisive factor in the choice of location is the prevailing wind direction. Can you be sure that the wind is not offshore, or will veer round to 'offshore' during the time spent on the water? Ideal conditions exist when the wind blows parallel to the shore (*side-shore*) or diagonal to the shore (*side onshore*). The location should of course also be suitable for the rider's level of ability. A beach with the wind blowing directly onshore should be avoided, as should stony beaches or those with obstacles in the water, such as platforms, for example.

■ **Tides:** The fact that the waves change with an incoming and an outgoing tide is not as critical as the fact that currents are often subject to strong variations due to the tidal range. Every water sports athlete should be well-informed on this subject, but especially kitesurfers, as they can lose manoeuvrability more quickly than others; it takes no more than a dropped kite for a kitesurfer to be driven quickly out into open sea. Anyone who isn't yet

able to go upwind satisfactorily should choose their starting point such that they can get back to this point in spite of strong currents, or can reach another safe location. If the current comes from the same direction as the wind, the kitesurfer drifts leeward, so that the apparent wind is weaker than the atmospheric wind. The speed of the current should therefore be subtracted from the wind velocity, thus a larger kite is required. If the conditions are reversed, then the kite chosen can suddenly be too big, something that poses similar hazards.

■ **Gear check and set-up** before starting: When inflating the kite, hold on to it firmly or attach it to the pump leash that is now fitted to nearly all pumps. Kites that fly away can not only become damaged, but can also pose a hazard to people. For this reason you should lay the kite down once you've inflated it, with the front tube into the wind, and weight it down with sufficient sand.

Before every kiting session special attention should be paid to attaching the lines. Even experienced kitesurfers have a mishap now and again that can prove fatal: they attach the lines incor-

rectly. This is why we strongly recommend that you 'run' the lines out, laying the central (*front* lines) between your legs and the *back* lines to right and left of your legs respectively.

Many kite manufacturers have now developed good systems that prevent incorrect line attachment, but there are others that haven't. Everyone should attach the lines in the manner he has learned or is accustomed to. On the bow kites that are frequently seen and used nowadays, however, a clearer arrangement is to run the lines out from the open side of the kite and attach them, so as not to get into a tangle with the *bridles*. If you lay the lines out from the open side of the kite, therefore, as Kristin is doing in the picture , you need to keep in mind that the *bar* is placed on the ground the

wrong way round, thus with the red side to the right, and this then has to be rotated 180 degrees upon launching the kite. The central lines between your legs are then fastened to the central *bridle* lines, and the outer lines to the outer attachment points. The danger of getting lines mixed up is reduced to a minimum in this way. Anyone who has already experienced a line break out at sea knows how dangerous and taxing the consequences can be. For this reason it is recommended that you check the lines and their attachment points to the kite and the *bar* carefully before every launch.

A foot strap that tears suddenly can cause serious injury to the knee and ankle joint of the leg that remains in the still-intact strap, because in the consequent fall that this triggers, the

012

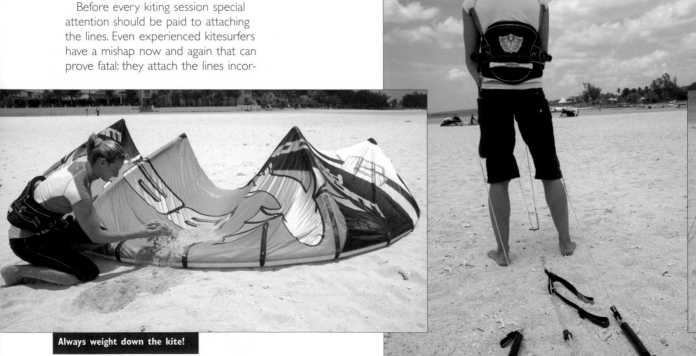

'Comb' the lines.

Always weight down the kite!

board acts with a full lever effect on the knee and/or ankle joint. So it's well worth carrying out a brief check of the foot-strap screws, as well as the webbing, prior to each launch.

■ **Thinking the launch through:** By this we mean the choice of launch position as well as the launch process itself. What's in the **leeward** direction? If something goes wrong, it's always in the leeward direction. If there are lots of people on the beach down wind of you, you should shift your launch position behind them for their protection. Other obstacles such as houses, pile dwellings, flagpoles, rocks etc. must be noted for your own protection and you should try to find a launch position that lies in the lee of these obstacles. In short, the beach must be free of people and obstructions for a sufficiently long distance downwind.

The kite must always be launched from the edge of the wind window, as it develops the least power here. If the kiter is going to launch, the safety leash and then the chicken loop should be hooked in first of all. Before finally launching, check once more whether the lines are fitted correctly and the bar is held the right way round. The

trimmer should be adjusted so as to launch with the minimum of power. After the kite has been released for launching by the person assisting, it must be steered slowly into the zenith to the neutral 12 o'clock position.

■ **Use the quick release as well!** This naturally presupposes that you are carrying a safety leash with you (see below). If a kitesurfer actually finds himself in a dangerous situation, everything happens very quickly, more often than not, too quickly for the quick release to be operated at all. We therefore advise that you double-check the quick-release function before each training session on the water. Furthermore, the actual release manoeuvre should be practised repeatedly, even if it results in having to sort the lines out. You have to know how to reach the quick release at all times.

■ **Right-of-way rules:** These apply to all sailing craft and thus also to kitesurfers. You should have a good grasp of these rules and keep them up to date:

1. **Starboard has right of way over port:** This rule is easy to remember, but the reformulated rule reads:

Always attach the lines carefully yourself!

Kite launch at the edge of the wind window.

The vessel with the wind blowing across the port side gives way to the vessel with the wind from the starboard side. This right-of-way protocol is relevant if two kiters or other sailing vessels are approaching one another. A rider on a port tack, thus flying his kite over the right-hand side of the board, must give way to an approaching kiter, windsurfer or sailing boat. A rider with his kite above the left-hand side of the board, and thus on a starboard tack, must keep his course.

The easiest way to remember this is as follows: A kiter who has his right hand forward on the *bar* has right of way over approaching vessels. A rider who has his left hand forward on the *bar* gives way.

2. **Leeward before windward**: This rule applies to two kitesurfers moving in the same direction. The kiter who is riding to windward, i.e. riding upwind of the other kiter, must give way. In most cases this means that he has to go to windward. The leeward craft must hold its course.

3. **Overtaking vessels keep clear**: Two line lengths are considered a safe distance in kiting!

4. If two kitesurfers are on the same course, then the upwind kiter pilots his kite **high** and the **downwind** rider flies his much **lower**. This prevents the kites from flying into one another.

5. The obligation to hold one's course in rules 1 to 3 doesn't mean that the course has to be maintained until a collision occurs. Here it's important to make the **'last-second manoeuvre'** required to avoid collision, even if the other vessel is obliged to give way but overlooks this.

6. An additional tip: Less experienced kitesurfers who are less familiar with the kite steering system, often steer their kite into the zenith when another kiter approaches. However, for the approaching kiter this is very awkward if he intends to pass upwind, as he cannot pilot his kite down. In this situation it is recommended to pilot the kite at least lower into the wind window edge, or simply to ride on, because the upwind kiter must keep clear!

■ **Knowledge of international kitesurfing signs**. The signs have been chosen so as to be independent of any specific language and so that they can be understood from some distance away:

Okay to launch:

Kristin gives a clearly visible 'thumbs up' sign to signal that everything is OK with her kite and it can be launched. The assistant confirms this with the same sign and releases the kite.

Help:

Kiters wave with both hands if possible, to signal that they need help.

014

Abort launch:

If Kristin realizes that something is wrong with her kite, she moves the flat of her hand back and forth in front of her throat, thereby signalling the launch is to be aborted.

Landing the kite:

Patting the head with the hand means that the rider wishes to land his kite. The assistant confirms this intention with the same sign.

Level of fitness: Unfortunately, it can be observed time and again that the length of the training session on the water doesn't match the level of fitness of the kiter. A lack of physical fitness can result in serious injuries. Worse still are the life-threatening situations that a water sports athlete can find himself in if his strength suddenly deserts him out on the water or he gets cramp. The time spent on the water should be gauged accordingly so that the rider returns to shore **before** he starts to feel tired. A good level of fitness extends the amount of time that can be spent on the water, and this level can be enhanced by suitable nutrition. This means taking on board sufficient carbohydrates and liquid far enough in advance of the training session.

Before embarking on a kitesurfing session in general, and especially prior to practising some tricks that put a particular strain on certain areas of the body – e.g. handlepasses, which stress the shoulder muscles – we recommend in principle that you strengthen the relevant muscles (see Chapter 9 "Training ashore – building up strength").

Don't just 'try out' new manoeuvres:, Visualize them effectively in advance and practise **mental imaging** (or training) (for more on this see Chapter 3 "Learn to kitesurf faster and better through mental imaging")!

Never go kiting alone! This point needs no further explanation.

Self-rescue: If an emergency should occur in spite of taking all safety precautions, e.g the rider aborts the action, the wind drops unexpectedly or problems occur with the equipment, such as broken lines, it's imperative that the kiter is able to save himself, because a rescue boat isn't always on hand. The decision regarding self-rescue should generally be taken in good time, to be precise as soon as the kiter aborts or is uncertain of a situation, because the opportunity must be taken while self-rescue is still possible.

The first element of self-rescue depends to some extent on the type of equipment. Some manufacturers fit their kites with a *grab handle* on one of the outer lines, and the kiter can use this to pull the kite towards him. However, the rider must let go of all the other lines and the *bar* completely (the rider must no longer be hooked in!), as otherwise the kite could develop power unintentionally. Other manufacturers have fitted the fifth line in such a way that the rider can use this to pull the kite towards him without any great effort. As soon as a rider who has got into difficulties has clung onto the kite, he can turn it over onto its back via the middle of the front tube and can swim back to the shore with board and kite. The leash can be used for assistance here by releasing it from the *bar* and hooking it to the middle of the front tube (e.g. at the attachment point for the 5th-line), enabling the rider to use both arms for swimming. In the best case scenario, when an onshore or side-onshore wind is blowing, the kite can also be used as a sail to pull the kiter ashore. This works better, however, if there is somewhat less air in the tube, so a little of the air must be let out. Doing this allows the kiter to pull both *tips* towards him and hold them in such a way that the kite fills with wind to some extent. The kiter can then let himself be pulled back to shore on a downwind reach with his kite in both hands. Sailing back in this way leaves no hands free for the board; the only possible means of bringing the board back is to lie on it, but it will be very wobbly with both hands on the kite. It is therefore advisable to practise this, as practising will reduce any fear of emergencies and increase your confidence.

If none of these self-rescue measures work and the land recedes further into the distance, your best option is to part with the kite and swim back with the board. In this case it should be considered whether this is actually possible, because if the rider were to be driven further out to sea, it would be highly sensible to hold onto the kite – on the one hand because it's a good buoyancy aid and on the other because it's easily visible from the air, e.g from a helicopter. There's no patent remedy for such situations; the right decision always depends on a number of factors, namely the wind, current, time of day, temperature, and the rider's physical condition and personal approach to handling such emergency situations. Before making a swift decision, the situation should be analysed briefly yet thoroughly to enable a good decision to be made as the rider sees fit.

Conclusion: It's worth being well prepared in every respect and also studying both the wind and weather conditions and the tide table carefully before venturing out onto the water. This enables riders to choose the location in a way that **avoids endangering either ourselves, or others.** After all, we are all responsible for acting with care to ensure that we don't jeopardize our sport!

Passive safety precautions

Generally speaking, passive safety precautions offer sensible protection. Think about the car air bag: it doesn't take an accident for the air bag to be seen as a sensible precaution. However, passive measures shouldn't be seen as opening the way to taking more risks.

■ **Helmet:** The risk of head injuries can be reduced by wearing a helmet – that's obvious. The secondary consequences of a head injury, on the other hand, aren't so obvious: it doesn't necessarily result in a loss of consciousness, but a reduced level of consciousness can have serious consequences. The injured rider is not only lying in the water, but in most cases is still suspended from the kite and could perform unintentional steering movements that could then catapult him all over the place.

■ **Impact jacket:** Painful bruised ribs can be caused by crashes when simply riding. This happens mostly if a sudden gust occurs when the rider is travelling at full speed and the kite is pulled forward forcefully. You don't have to experience at first hand how painful and restrictive this injury can be before deciding to wear an impact jacket. In normal jumps and especially in rotation jumps – even more so with kiteloops – the danger of bruising the ribs is far greater. The accelerated impact on the surface of the water can easily cause ribs to be broken. This is not only extremely painful, but can also be life-threatening if a broken rib punctures the pleura or lung.

The safety leash should be attached to the harness at the back so as to give maximum freedom of movement. Using these two safety devices is a must and they should naturally be checked before each start to ensure that they function properly. The leash is essential particularly with regard to the safety of other kiters, because in most cases a rider who triggers the quick release will become separated from his kite. Without a safety leash the kite could fly into other kiters, or even become entangled in their lines. The use of a safety leash is therefore necessary to prevent a rider from losing his own kite and especially in order not to endanger other kiters! Since each manufacturer has a different method of attaching the leash to the bar, it's important to familiarize yourself well with the method of attachment before using the kite.

■ **Board leash:** This offers security – in the sense that the kitesurfer can recover his board more quickly in a fall – and poses a hazard at the same time, because when the rider takes a tumble, the board leash can tighten sharply, causing it to act like an elastic band and catapult the board into the back of the rider. Going upwind by *body dragging* should therefore be incorporated into the training programme at an early stage, so that the board leash can be removed at the earliest possible opportunity. If you use a leash nevertheless a helmet and impact jacket should always be worn too!

Conclusion: As long as the helmet and impact jacket aren't abused as a 'free licence' for the kiter to perform inappropriate, reckless and risky manoeuvres, these safety measures above are as much to be recommended as the established safety systems on kites.

The safety system consists of the quick release and safety leash.

2 Choosing your training content

Of course, you can simply go kitesurfing without giving any thought as to what you could practise out on the water, but then you run the risk of missing something. And who willingly passes up the opportunity of an experience? We advise that, before going out on the water and after you've weighed up the conditions, you give some consideration to which of your skills might suit the prevailing wind and wave conditions and could then be practised.

Kitesurfing: a *flow* experience

Everyone who indulges in a particular sport has his reasons, and, in the case of extreme sports at least, these are often pretty similar; in kitesurfing as in other such sports, the participant experiences a euphoric sensation that fills him with a deep sense of satisfaction. Attaining this sensation can be the reason for indulging in the sport, and one quickly gets the feeling that a structured training programme might be at odds with this. Wrong! The opposite may even be the case. At the start of the twentieth century, Groos (1901; see Bibliography) answered the question posed above with the term *"Funktionslust"* – man's pleasure in functioning is satisfied when the body functions in harmony with its physical and sensory potential. Here freedom is the decisive criterion of a joyous action in which the participant loses himself completely. Now, many years down the line, this euphoric state or experience is termed *flow*. According to this theory, the participant loses himself entirely in the flow of his actions; he kites for hours over the sea and is oblivious to the passage of time, he is totally focused on the here and now. "In

a state of *flow*, one action follows another according to an inner logic that appears to require no conscious intervention on the part of the participant" (Csikszentmihalyl, 1999: p. 59). The participant is scarcely aware of the divide between himself and his environment. To use a cliché, the kitesurfer is at one with the sea and the wind in these moments. But what does

that mean with regard to training tips for kitesurfers?

It's perfectly possible to support the attainment of this *flow* state, but it's important to know what conditions produce it; one's own capabilities must match the challenge of the situation, (Csikszentmihalyl, 1999: p. 62: "Flow only seems to occur if the challenge lies within the range of capability of the individual"), so that the participant feels neither anxiety nor boredom. This means that the wind and wave conditions should be chosen so as to produce this balance. Of course, this is rather difficult, because unfortunately – or perhaps fortunately – we cannot choose the wind and weather conditions. However, the training programme can and should be designed according to the external conditions thereby ensuring that the level of ability is precisely coordinated to the demands of the situation. On a day with good waves and a side-shore wind, for example, it makes sense to choose a small kite and practise wave riding downwind, whereas on another day with little wind and flat water, it's sensible to choose a big kite, which is stable in the air and won't react to the smallest steering movements, to practise one's first rotation jumps etc. In this way even in a simple training process, action and consciousness are fused and thus become a *flow* experience. And we all know that incredibly good feeling we get when a jump or manoeuvre that we've just been practising suddenly goes right: these are the special moments in which we are 'in the zone'. And for these, it's always worth thinking things through a little in advance.

This training programme is structured so that its content capitalizes on one's existing abilities, thus not too difficult but not too easy either. This way, the choice of training content produces a pleasant sensation of energy and relaxation at the same time, which in turn boosts motivation.

> **Conclusion:** The contents of the training session should be chosen carefully taking one's own ability and the prevailing external conditions into consideration!

The question of motivation

Extreme sports athletes, who often have to endure difficult circumstances to be able to pursue their sport, are motivated enough. At least, one would think so. But this extra energy, which we are aware of and which propels us that bit further forward or higher, is what we sometimes need. The key lies in choosing what is to be practised, in order to attain the *flow* experience described above on the one hand, and on the other hand to facilitate the highest possible level of motivation and thus the supply of energy. The level of difficulty of the training content should lie in the medium range; if it is well beyond one's capabilities, then a sense of resignation or even feelings of anxiety may arise, which can in turn become dangerous – because extreme anxiety results in blockages. However, if the situation presents such a challenge that it prompts a tinge of fear now and again, this immediately signals to the athlete that he must exert himself considerably, which results in turn in good learning progress. Training content that is too easy, on the other hand, can result in a lack of concentration and can therefore be just as hazardous as training content that is too difficult.

When setting your learning goals, you need to bear in mind that goals that are too remote, or even unattainable, give rise to a sense of resignation. So it makes sense to set medium-term goals that are achievable. These should build on one another and thereby ensure adequate motivation.

> **Conclusion:** Each training session on the water should pose a suitably measured challenge matched to one's level of ability and to the external conditions: **"Don't demand too much – but stimulate!"** (Hossner, 1993: p. 20).

Structuring a training unit

In nearly all types of sport, the training has a structured content geared both to the ability and physical condition of the individual and to knowledge derived from sports and coaching science. The fact that many extreme sports athletes do not apply this structure to their sports discipline is an omission. Anyone who goes kitesurfing without going about it in an organized manner will learn something each time, but won't attain the success that could be achieved. To optimize training and accelerate one's learning progress, the tips from the preceding and following sections should

be borne in mind. In this section we once more bring together all aspects in relation to a training unit and we've also added a number of other points that should be considered.

Time on the water

We have often observed that sessions on the water are far too long. The time spent on the water should always match the rider's level of fitness (for more about fitness, see Chapter 9), and therefore should only last as long as the rider has sufficient stamina, as otherwise over-training effects can occur, and by the end of the session the tricks no longer succeed as well as they might. This is due to the fact that the muscles fail to perform as well after a certain time, as does the neuromuscular system, i.e. one's coordination becomes poorer. The time spent in kitesurfing can be extended considerably by making sure you take breaks in which you eat something, but above all, you need to drink enough. The time on the water should not be much more than an hour at a time when riding intensely.

Variety and two-sidedness

What a pity it would be if you're only able to perform certain tricks in one direction and in certain conditions. One of many theories regarding motor learning states that training the second-best side of the body also optimizes coordination on the better side of the body. This is due less to the fact that the motor centre of the left-hand side of the body lies in the right hemisphere of the brain, and that of the right-hand side of the body lies in the left hemisphere of the brain, than to the fact that the two hemispheres of the brain are cross-linked. By practising on the side that isn't so good, one's awareness of the movement is advanced, which in turn helps to prevent the formation of a so-called 'best side' and assists more in varying the execution of manoeuvres and making this execution steadier on both sides. Tricks

also become more consistent in execution if practised in changing conditions, meaning in different wind/wave configurations. You should therefore always practise a new trick on both sides and in a variety of conditions!

Furthermore, tricks performed with the 'reverse side', thus in *switch* mode, score more points in a competition.

Following up the training session on the water

After the training session on the water, it makes sense to go over it and consider what worked well and what wasn't so good. The results are processed for further practical training sessions in advance using mental imaging (or training), in the sense that changes in the execution of the trick are incorporated into the 'mental film'. The rider then rehearses this repeatedly before the trick is next performed.

The advice for optimizing kitesurfing training that we've given so far and is detailed further below and provides a structure for the content of the training. We recommend **training in seven phases** in principle:

1 Selection of training content (see Chapter 2).

2 **Mental imaging** (see Chapter 3).

3 **Warming up** (see Chapter 4).

4 **Getting in the mood/activation** (see Chapters 4 and 5).

5 **Training on the water** (see Chapters 5 and 6).

6 **Cool down** (see Chapter 7).

7 **Follow-up** (see Chapter 2).

3 Learning to kitesurf faster and better through mental imaging

In the television coverage of the last 2006 Winter Olympics, the bobsleigh riders could be seen just before the start of the race standing on the run with eyes closed, turning their head first quickly to the right, then more slowly to the left. These head movements of varying intensity and speed quite simply represent the radius of the curve that they were just passing through in their imagination. In advance of the actual race, bobsleigh riders travel the entire run in their head in real time. There are many other instances in sports too, from pole-vaulting to teeing off in golf, in which this additional form of training has long since become firmly established. And it should be the same in kitesurfing, because "the virtually classic application (of mental imaging)" is ascribed to kitesurfing as one of the 'sports with complex, highly coordinated movements that are also geared to precision and short decision-making moments' (Gabler, Hauser, Hug & Steiner, 1985: p. 235). Imagine a trick such as the 'One foot 360°', which is difficult to coordinate owing to its complexity. Moreover, it isn't possible, for example, to perform just a part of a 360, a handlepass or a kiteloop; it's either all or nothing. If undertaken properly and in peace, mental imaging helps to convey the sensation of having already experienced the new trick that one wishes to practise. As such it's ideally suited to reinforcing learning and training processes in kitesurfing.

Kristin during mental imaging immediately prior to training on the water.

Kristin Boese, the 2005, 2006 and 2007 world champion, always uses forms of mental imaging when she wishes to learn new tricks or to refine highly complex jumps that she has already mastered, to make them more reliable, or to transfer them to other conditions. Mental imaging supports learning processes at all levels, from beginner to world champion.

Clarifying the concept: What is mental imaging?

Mental imaging is "learning and/or improving a movement sequence by means of intensive visualisation without simultaneous realisation of the movement visualised". (Tiwald, 1973: p. 57). Volpert describes mental imaging in a similar manner as "the systematically repeated, deliberate visualisation of a sporting action without its simultaneous practical execution" (Volpert, 1976: p. 66). The aim is to simplify the learning of a movement in a new sport by creating an image of the movement, or to achieve an improvement in the practical movement by improving the image. It could also be described simply as "internal rehearsal" (Tiwald, 1973: p. 57). Mental imaging can also help to reduce anxiety.

Mental imaging cannot take the place of practical training sessions, but it can underpin them, because in the course of the learning process, the movement image becomes increasingly differentiated on account of the feedback from practical training that is also incorporated into the mental picture. This method yields success more quickly than pure trial and error or external correction, which does not affect one's own movement image, but rather someone else's, namely, that of the person doing the correcting.

Prerequisites for mental imaging

General prerequisites

One particular prerequisite for mental imaging is a positive attitude to the method. Mental imaging is also only possible if the trainee is in a "state of relative relaxation" (Eberspächer, 1990: p. 76). This is because optimum visualization intensity can only be attained by someone who is in a mentally and physically relaxed state overall. There are plenty of options for achieving this state of relaxation such as: listening to relaxing music or performing breathing exercises. One breathing exercise, for example, consists in assuming a relaxed sitting or lying posture, breathing out emphatically four or five times and falling in with this breathing rhythm, concentrating as one does so on the abdominal area and thinking 'in' when breathing in and 'out' when breathing out; distractions are thereby shut out, which in turn induces a relaxed state.

Visualization: creating movement imagery

The visualization itself is preceded first by familiarization with the objective: what should the mental imaging focus on? It's important here to restrict yourself to one trick that is to be learned. The subsequent production of the movement image is the theoretical reproduction of an image of a movement stored in the memory. This image should reflect the overall complexity and the dynamic, temporal and spatial relationships between the elements of a trick. To this end it makes sense to try and gain an in-depth understanding of the tricks illustrated in the section "Training on the water", which we discuss further in Chapter 6. The photo sequences have been selected so that all the basic elements of a trick can be understood, an essential prerequisite for the success of the mental imaging. When developing movement imagery as a basis for the mental imaging session, it's advisable to include as many senses as possible (cf. Syer & Connolly, 1984: p. 53): we need the kinaesthetic sense (consisting of neuromuscular spindles, joint and tendon receptors) just as we need the sense of balance – these two together provide information on the position of the body in space – and the visual sense. The more intensively the different levels of perception are combined to produce an integrated movement sensation, the greater the value acquired by the movement imagery (cf. Syer & Connolly, 1984: p. 54). The accuracy of the elements of a trick 'developed' in the visualization process determines how helpful the visualization really is out on the water later, as it's then possible to revert quickly to the internal images and perceptions. "in other words, if you visualise yourself moving, you may see, hear and feel yourself moving" (Syer & Connolly, 1984) If a good, vivid image of the situation works, then physical reactions such as the heart pounding and increased muscle tone will occur. The trainee thus has the opportunity to become accustomed to the situation that will arise frequently later on the water.

The movement image must also be formulated in the athlete's own words and be oriented to the individual's actual situation, i.e. the goals set must be attainable. In addition, the trainee should attempt to visualize the situation and the tricks as vividly as possible from his own as well as from the external perspective. The choice of perspective depends on the type of mental imaging selected.

Types of mental imaging

It has proved highly advisable to differentiate clearly between the following types of mental imaging and not to mix them up, as different perception systems are addressed. We recommend subvocal training as an introduction; for those who already have experience of mental imaging, the other two types are equally suitable.

Subvocal training

In this type of mental imaging, the trainee visualises the trick through self-talk. The photo sequences in Chapter 6 'Basics and Tricks' serve as a description, which has to be graphic and in which key points are specially highlighted. In the chapter, the decisive moments in each trick are named and formulations are suggested for these key points. To perform the mental imaging, however, these should be put into one's own words.

Concealed perception training

In concealed perception training, the trainee observes himself from an external perspective. In his mind he plays a film of his own movements. The visualisation of a successful trick or a change in an existing movement image can be backed up by the photo sequences in Part II. When watching an 'inner film' of a trick repeatedly, the trainee should focus his attention specifically on various key points of the action.

Both sub-vocal training and concealed perception training are more strongly controlled from outside. When learning complex tricks, the following type of training has proved best.

Ideomotor training

For this form of mental imaging it is necessary to envisage the situation in which the action takes place in the present. In doing this, it's imperative to shut out any anxiety that might arise in the real situation, as otherwise this becomes a permanent element of the action. The athlete puts himself mentally into the situation and emulates the inner processes that take place when performing the corresponding motions. If executed properly, this can even result in the muscles being activated in the way in which they are involved in the target movement, albeit to a smaller extent. "When you imagine yourself moving, the muscle groups involved in such an action actually move on a subliminal level" (Syer & Connolly, 1984; p, 48) According to Tiwald (1973: p. 57), mental imaging can also be described as "action with an inhibited final motor link" on account of this fact. This effect of mental imaging is termed the 'Carpenter effect' or also, 'ideomotor micromovements'. (Tiwald, 1973: p. 196). During intensive visualization, an increased supply of blood and acceleration of the breathing and heart rate have also been shown to occur.

The crucial criterion for effective mental imaging is accordingly the ability both to visualize the trick vividly and to develop the strength-dynamic components via inner perception (here in particular due to the kinaesthetic and balance sense) by repeated practice.

Both the choice of internal perspective and that of external perspective are equally sensible in mental imaging. The choice of perspective is dictated by the so-called primary sense of each individual. Those who choose the external perspective are more visually oriented, while those who opt for the internal perspective are more kinaesthetically oriented. The choice of perspective should be left up to the individual, and

023

then the perspectives should be swapped later in training.

Carrying out a mental imaging session

Mental imaging sessions are linked to the practical sessions on the water, i.e. mental imaging is used to prepare for and review the practical session on the water. The mental imaging itself is undertaken in four stages.

Stage 1: The trainee describes the trick to be practised in his own words in the present, drawing on as many senses as possible. In this way the consciousness content is structured in relation to the target action.

Stage 2: The entire action sequence (e.g. the backflip below) is visualised through self-talk. The trainee talks through the trick for himself. In this process, it's not yet important for the mental and practical execution to coincide in terms of time; in fact, the entire movement sequence should be observed in the manner of an 'internal slow-motion film'. (Syer and Connolly (1984: pp. 54–55) state that "there are two occasions when you should slow your mental rehearsal down. The first is when you set up the rehearsal programme".) In this way it becomes possible to record everything that makes up the action in the backflip and integrate it into the 'internal film'.

Realising this subvocal image smoothly is an essential condition for the third stage, because it prevents disruptions such as counter- images (e.g. the unsuccessful execution of a trick), thinking blocks and rewinding and repeating in the 'internal film'.

Stage 3: The key points of the trick as a whole should be highlighted, i.e. the elements of the overall action sequence are systematized. Key points are the crucial five or six points in the trick. These key points are marked. For the

024

backflip, the following key points are conceivable:

1. Kite at 11 o'clock or 1 o'clock, place hands close together.
2. Go upwind and pop with the back leg.
3. Start to rotate, aid rotation by head movement.
4. Bend legs, look over shoulder and complete rotation.
5. Extend legs and fix landing point.
6. Absorb landing.

The 'internal film' is abridged by the symbolic marking, so that the 'film' takes up a similar length of time as it does when performing the movement in practice.

Stage 4: Thanks to further symbolic marking, these summarized key points can be called up both during the mental and the practical execution of the movement. The following symbols could be used for the backflip:

1. 'Hands'
2. 'Go upwind … and pop'
3. 'R-o-t-a-t-e'
4. 'Minimize "'
5. 'Extend legs'
6. 'Absorb landing'

The degree of expansion or compression of the symbolized key points should help to support the rhythm of the trick and to achieve a correspondence in time of the mental and practical execution. If the movement is carried out more slowly in the visualization than in the real situation, it will then be executed too slowly in practice, which results in falls.

A mental imaging session should be interrupted after three to five minutes on one item for relaxation between the 'films', as the full concentration that is required for visualization can scarcely be maintained for longer than this. The visualization should be concluded with the trainee seeing himself performing a trick in which everything goes to plan.

Effects of mental imaging

'Mentally experiencing' a complex trick in kitesurfing produces a familiarity with this situation that helps the trainee in the practical situation on the water. In the optimum case, learners who are out on the water have already repeatedly experienced and mastered the situation in which they then find themselves. Due to this so-called "reliability of action" (Gabler, Hauser, Hug & Steiner, 1985: p. 228) a reduction in anxiety is achieved in addition to an improvement in the action. The danger of a block resulting from anxiety is thus reduced.

A further effect of mental imaging is that, due to intensive visualization, the interaction between consciousness and muscle system is improved and thus specific movement images are optimally converted into corresponding muscle activity. it's important to strive to be 'at one' with the athletic motion accomplished, to which end "the visualisation of one's own optimum movement action has been 'integrated' so thoroughly and deeply into the organism and its control system that a minimum of friction or loss of the energy to be used to correct deviations occurs in the actual performance of the movement." (Gabler, Hauser, Hug & Steiner, 1985: p. 224) This is predomi-

nantly attributable to the Carpenter effect already described above.

Negative effects arise in mental imaging when learning a new trick if unintentional images refer to faulty movements, thus to unsuccessful tricks. These should be avoided at all costs.

Conclusion: Carried out properly and in peace, mental imaging offers a superb option for intensifying training processes in kitesurfing and thus optimizing one's ability – because those people using mental imaging can really feel how they perform a new trick in the scene visualized.

4 'Warming up': warm-up and activation phase before kiting

In nearly all sports, it's normal practice to devote time to an extensive warming-up programme. Only among windsurfers and kitesurfers, word hasn't got around yet that this type of preparation is sensible, or even necessary. Very high stresses are put on the ligaments, joints and muscles in kitesurfing. To avoid both serious injuries and long-term damage, the following training advice should be heeded.

General warm-up phase

Sensible preparation begins with preparation of the whole body specific to the type of sport. In addition to tuning up the cardiovascular system, the 'warm-up' is especially important for the joint structures: A joint must be moved for at least 5 five minutes to enable increased synovial fluid to be produced.' (Buchbauer, 2001: p. 34). Ten minutes of warming up increases the fluid take-up of the cartilage due to an increase in its thickness, resulting in an improved buffer function in the knee joint. It is only in this way that tendons and joints can be prepared for the considerable load imposed by kitesurfing. (A body temperature of 39–40° is recognized as optimum, as the best elasticity of the collagen structures prevails at this temperature. At low temperatures with an inadequate neoprene suit, kiting is accordingly harmful to the ligaments and joints.) We recommend a loose, **ten-minute limbering-up session** followed by loose **circling of the arms, torso and shoulders in both directions.** This produces the mobility required for kiting and also increases the nerve conduction velocity, which markedly improves coordination. And good coordination is an essential

prerequisite for kitesurfing, as described in Chapter 8. Furthermore, warming up prepares the cardiovascular system for the load that will be imposed on it and the increased metabolism required, which simply works better at a higher temperature; muscles that have been warmed up satisfactorily don't experience overacidity so quickly.

A brief note on **stretching**: the effectiveness of stretching as a preparation for training to prevent injury and to avoid muscular imbalance (e.g. between the back and stomach muscles) has not been proven. (It was overvalued for years and replaced a sport-specific warm-up for many leisure sports enthusiasts.) It's therefore not necessary to stretch before a session on the water.

Kitesurfing-specific activation phase

Kitesurfing calls for one's level of perception and coordinative abilities to be well developed. Naturally every kitesurfer already has these attributes to a differing degree, depending on their previous experience. A good skateboarder, for example, already has considerable balancing ability, which will make it much easier for him to pick up the new sport (see Chapter 8 for the crossover effect). Nevertheless, every athlete who is 'pre-trained' in this manner, or is a good athlete in any case, should work on developing his skills further. Of course, this can be achieved simply by practising the sport, but it can be accelerated or optimized substantially by performing special exercises. Carried out before each training session on the water, these exercises also activate one's system for the kiting to follow. After all, professional

footballers or basketball players don't just play their own game in training; they also do exercises that develop their general and specific skills further. So why not do the same in kitesurfing? Various exercises have proved useful:

1. In order to **activate** and practise the **balancing ability,** which is drawn on heavily in kitesurfing, it has proved extremely useful to 'wake up' the pertinent system first while still ashore. In the first stage, the trainee stands on one leg and tries to maintain his balance. This is made more difficult if he shuts his eyes. He then takes his hands out of the balance equation by putting them in his pockets or placing them behind his back. Those who are experienced at balancing will not have any problem even with the most difficult stage in this exercise, which can be performed any time and does not call for any equipment: the raised leg is rested on the knee of the standing leg, the eyes remain closed and the hands remain in the pockets. (Further exercises can be found under "Neuromuscular training" in Chapter 9 and in the literature quoted.)

   In her training Kristin often resorts to balancing exercises from yoga, and these are also highly recommended.

2. An exercise for **getting warm and activating the hips and legs** consists of bouncing lightly from a position identical to the position on the board, as if one were intending to cushion the board. This can be taken to the next level by rotating in the jump, first with one's eyes open, then with them closed. Attention should be paid during

this manoeuvre to a good landing with appropriate cushioning with the knees. One's **orientation ability** can also be activated by estimating the amount of rotation achieved after turning with one's eyes shut.

3. Another exercise eminently suitable for kiting is **activation of the shoulder muscles** with the aid of a *bar* attached to a tree. It's possible to hook the harness into this so that preparatory exercises geared to the contents of the training session on the water can be carried out. Normal riding with steering movements can be imitated, as can rotation jumps or pulling up the board etc. This will also help to get you suitably **attuned for the kiting session.**

4. Exercise for **developing a feel for the kite**: always knowing the position of the kite in the air at all times, without having to look at it, is essential, as the rider should be free to keep his eyes on the surface of the water. One exercise consists of steering the kite in flat water with one's eyes closed when there is little wind. The effect of this exercise is that the pressure which the kite generates in different positions is associated with a stimulus that is perceived via the muscle kinaesthesia (kinaesthetic analyser) due to the sense of sight being switched off; the kite is thus not seen, but felt.

Conclusion: By spending 15 to 20 minutes on the warm-up and activation phase and going out onto the water properly warmed up and prepared, the rider will not only kite better, but will be able to kite for longer and will not suffer injuries and overload damage as quickly.

TRAINING ON

Following suitable preparation, it's now time to go on the water. First we show exercises that activate and practise the general skills required for kiting, followed by the basics and then, ordered according to their degree of difficulty, various tricks. The descriptions in conjunction with the photographs should help to form the movement imagery required for mental imaging.

5 Specific warm-up on the water

In addition to the special warm-up, the following exercises focus on developing a feel for the kite, the board and the elements. Because in their daily lives people are geared to using sight as their primary sense, this characteristic is naturally carried over to sport, something that often runs counter to the requirements of the sport. Here's an example: in everyday existence, vertical structures that provide us with constant information on the direction of gravity help us to maintain our balance, although other senses (namely the vestibular sense interacting with the kinaesthetic sense), are actually responsible for this. In both windsurfing and kitesurfing, the horizon as a known constant helps us to keep our balance. Due to this, our sense of balance doesn't have to work so hard for us, we relieve our sense of balance of a portion of its work, which unfortunately also robs it of some of its potential; because the more highly developed our balancing skill, the better and safer our performance. It's obvious that exercises in which the visual sense is switched off enhance and

improve balance. We have already described the exercises to be carried out ashore. With regard to the exercises that should be carried out on the water, you should ensure that the stretch of water is known, flat and above all completely clear, because for a couple of seconds one's eyes are fixed directly on the surface of the water, causing the horizon as a fixed constant to be lost from the field of vision, or the eyes are briefly closed. Before carrying out these exercises, a brief 'running-in' session on the water is advised. This should be undertaken loosely and with as little power as possible initially. To achieve good **mobility,** move your arms in a circular motion and your torso loosely back and forth.

Kite control exercises: Apart from a clear, flat stretch of water, a kite that is small in relation to the wind is needed for this exercise. The board should be kept on a straight course, with the rider looking first directly ahead of the board at the surface of the water, or with his eyes closed for a couple of seconds. Then the kite is steered cautiously back and

forth. Full attention should be paid to the kite when doing this, as it will improve the rider's feel for the board.

Developing a **feel for the board:** The aim is to ride on a clear stretch of water with one's eyes closed for a brief moment. The kiter should concentrate solely on his board while doing this and sense the board in all its movements. The effect of this exercise is to improve perception of the board and the resulting ability to control the board well, and above all in a manner appropriate to the situation.

Balance exercises: In order to visualize the shift in weight when travelling in a curve, the rider imagines himself negotiating a slalom course. Practising quick edge changing not only helps when going upwind and bearing away, which is what the exercise actually comprises, but also in many manoeuvres such as jibing, for example, or riding waves. Again, this exercise can be made more difficult by performing it on a flat, clear stretch of water with eyes closed for a brief moment. To prevent the development of

THE WATER

a 'best' side, the exercise should be carried out on both courses.

Exercises for controlling the kite in a kiteloop on various courses: The rider should start on a broad reach course directly after bearing away, as the kite pressure is then relatively light. This exercise develops the ability to handle different positions and thus power levels of the kite and to counterbalance these with the board. It's also a good preliminary exercise for the kiteloop itself. In this exercise the rider should take care to ride sufficiently 'behind the kite', which ensures that the pressure remains relatively light.

Practice jumps: At the end of the activation phase on the water, easy jumps are practised and the degree of difficulty of these is slowly increased up to the jump that is to be practised. By doing this the rider achieves both fine-tuning of the movements and toning of the muscles, enabling muscles to contract more quickly and thus in turn protect the joints.

This selection of exercises can be expanded in any way you like, but as with the exercises described above, it is very important to take care that no other kiters are put at risk and that you always

keep a sufficient distance away from other people and objects! You can give free rein to your imagination. Selected exercises should be incorporated regularly into the training session or used to activate the body and the central nervous system, particularly in this case, for the tasks ahead. In addition, the rider needs to visualize the sequence of the trick to be practised, which has been embedded satisfactorily in mental imaging (or training), before performing it for the first time.

6 Basics and tricks

In this chapter we present a selection of riding techniques that build on one another, starting with the basic riding technique, the water start, and extending to the first aerial handlepass, and riding waves. Unfortunately not all tricks can be included, so we have restricted ourselves to a selection of the main ones.

In the descriptions, the position of the kite in the air is indicated using the 'clock system' familiar from kite schools. It should be noted that this is always done from the viewpoint of the rider. Where Kristin is pictured facing the reader, you need to turn the pictures round. To produce good movement imagery, we advise that you try and gain an in-depth understanding of the trick with regard to the different perspectives. (See Chapter 4 "Learning to kitesurf faster and better through mental imaging".)

The key points required for mental imaging are included with the illustrations and descriptions of the riding techniques. The 'symbolic markings' are deliberately not given, as they must be coined in the trainee's own words for the mental imaging to be effective.

The tricks are illustrated and explained in their simplest form. Once a trick has

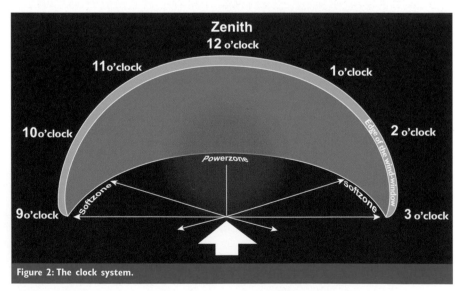

Figure 2: The clock system.

been mastered, the rider can then work on the execution and style (e.g. position of the kite, other grabs etc.).

Basics

As already clarified at the beginning, this training programme is by no means intended as a substitute for the first stages of instruction at a kite school! In this section we touch only briefly on aspects of kite school instruction as a reminder, but we certainly recommend such instruction as an introduction to the sport. Techniques such as *riding switch* and *riding blind*, which go beyond this level and form the basis for more advanced tricks, are also shown in this chapter.

- Body drag
- Water start
- Riding
- Going upwind and riding positions
- Steering with the board
- Riding switch
- Riding blind

Starting and riding

Body drag

As stated in Chapter 1, kitesurfing without a board leash is not as dangerous as kiting with one. So in order not to lose your board if you crash, it's advisable to be able to tack in deep water, hanging on to the kite.

To 'drag' upwind as effectively as possible, Kristin straightens out her body by stretching her legs out behind her and extending her lower arm well out in front, so that she counteracts the leeway with her body. The body practically assumes the function of a fin in the water, and the head can be rested on the arm while doing this. To change course, Kristin bends her legs to retain control of her body and steers the kite slowly through the zenith; this prevents her from being lifted out of the water, which would cause her to be carried back downwind again. The kite has to be steered with one hand when body dragging. This is best done with the hand placed in the centre of the *bar*.

Tip: Once you've mastered the art of *body dragging*, it's even possible to go upwind better in this way than riding on the board. *Body dragging* can also be especially useful if the wind drops so much that kiting back to the shore is no longer possible due to the lack of power. To do this, simply remove the board from your feet, then press it into the water with the front hand so that the board edge counters the leeway. Body dragging with the board can also help to get through big shore breaks and other difficult conditions. In a shore break the waves break directly onto the beach.

Water start

The water start is the simplest and surest way of getting onto the board. It can be refined depending on the wind strength: if there is little wind, for example, the kite must be steered far enough back into the opposite direction you intend to ride in order to then fly it deeper through the power zone. In this water start, these steering movements are a little less strong, as Kristin has sufficient power in the kite.

Floating in the water and holding the kite in the zenith with her rear hand on the centre of the *bar*, Kristin first aligns her board in the riding direction. Then she places her feet in the foot-straps and bends her legs. So as not to drift to leeward while in the water and to retain better board and body control, she edges her board sharply. Then she steers her kite opposite to the riding direction back to the 11 o'clock position and gains momentum in this way. With her front hand she pulls the kite into the soft zone, keeping her centre of gravity well back as a counterweight to the pull of the kite, pulls herself onto the board and then stands up actively using her back leg. She turns her upper body in the direction in which she is riding, travelling initially on a broad reach. In doing so she straightens her front leg as much as possible and flexes her back leg. Once riding steadily, she can put more pressure on the heel-side in order to go upwind and ride her desired course.

Key points for mental imaging:
- Hold the bar in the centre and kite to 12 o'clock
- Pull board towards you with one hand
- Feet into straps and draw up knees
- Steer kite back to 11 or 1 o'clock and then fly it through the soft zone
- Stand up as kite gains power
- Put pressure on heelside at the rear
- Extend front leg.

Tip: As soon as you have learnt how to steer the kite satisfactorily and can control it well, it's advisable to kitesurf with adequate power. This makes both the water start and riding away easier, as there's no need to fly the kite up and down as much.

Riding

If the water start is successful, the rider will find himself on a reach to begin with. In light wind it's necessary to fly the kite in a sweeping **pattern (flying figure eights).** The air flow against the kite is amplified by the increasing head wind and thus the speed increases. As the riding speed increases, the figure eights become smaller until they are no longer necessary to gain power and the rider is travelling fast enough.

When there is little wind and low kite power, the board can only be edged at intervals. When flying the kite up from the 9:30 position, Kristin depowers her kite by extending her arms and takes a little pressure off the board edge. She flies the kite up to the 11 o'clock position and then back down again. When flying the kite down, she *powers* it by pulling on the *bar*, and edges the board.

Tip: The kite builds up most pressure when flying downwards or upwards, not at the highest and the lowest point. To make flying in figure eights efficient, the kite should be flown as quickly as possible, so as to minimize the moments in which the kite builds up little pressure.

Key points for mental imaging:
- Fly kite down into the 9:30 or 2:30 position
- Power kite while doing so and edge the board
- Fly kite up to 11 or 1 o'clock
- Ease off the board edge and depower the kite
- Steer kite in riding direction again …

Wind window when stationary.

If the wind is strong enough, no sweeping pattern is necessary; the kite flies in a fixed position at roughly 45°. The wind window ashore is different from that experienced when riding, as on land only the atmospheric 'true' wind is effective.

On the water, the wind conditions change as the speed increases: the head wind increases, so that the apparent wind is further forward of the beam, i.e. it comes more from the riding direction.

The consequence of this is that the kite automatically flies deeper into the wind window, which increases the pressure and thus the speed. This can have the effect that the kitesurfer bears ever further away at high speed and can no longer control the board. The remedy in this situation is first to follow the kite, which takes the pressure out of it, and while doing so to steer the kite up into the zenith. To avoid getting into this situa-

tion, it's advisable to apply pressure to the heelside as soon as the speed increases and to go to windward. The effect is that the head wind migrates in the direction of the atmospheric wind, which also shifts the apparent wind in the same direction, i.e. it veers aft. This gives rise to a close reach; the kiter is thus riding diagonally 'towards the wind'. This course enables the kitesurfer to go upwind.

Figure 3: Change in kite position and wind window due to head wind.

Going upwind

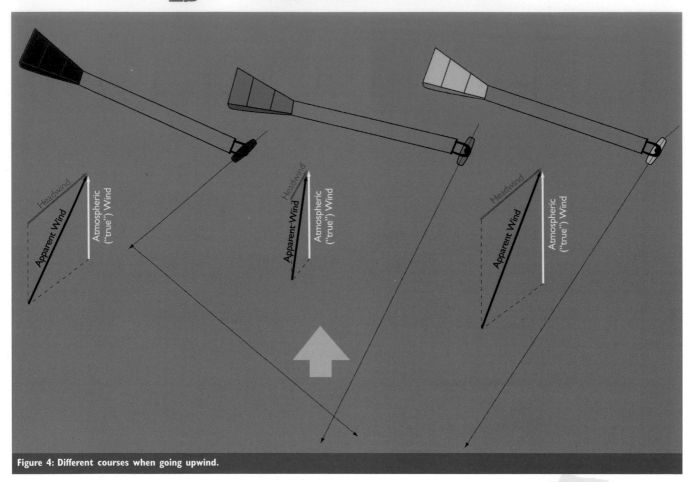

Headwind
Apparent Wind
Atmospheric ("true") Wind

Headwind
Apparent Wind
Atmospheric ("true") Wind

Headwind
Apparent Wind
Atmospheric ("true") Wind

Figure 4: Different courses when going upwind.

Being able to go upwind is a basic prerequisite for kitesurfing, because you can only kite if you can go upwind and thus get back to where you started from. To achieve this, it helps to have a clear understanding of the following interrelationships.

The red kiter is riding quite fast close to the wind, thus producing a relatively strong head wind, which causes the apparent wind to move further forward of the beam. His course is thus not closest to the wind, but due to the fact

that this kiter is riding faster, he "sails the best course to windward" (Overschmidt & Gliewe, 2004: p. 46) – he is gaining the most ground. The green kiter is **'pointing high'**, i.e. he takes speed out of his board by edging sharply, due to which the apparent wind is more abaft, i.e. it comes more from the direction of the 'true wind'. The result is a maximum close-hauled course, but it's slower.

The yellow kiter experiences a sudden gust or the wind picks up quickly. In this case, the stronger atmospheric wind

changes the apparent wind to the effect that this is further abaft. The kiter can take advantage of this and fly the kite further to windward, as the wind window 'opens' due to the stronger wind. The result is that he can point high, as the angle to the wind is favourable and the speed remains high. This also means in turn that to be able to go upwind easily a sufficiently large kite should always be chosen, but never one that is too big.

On a close reach, which is the course ridden when going upwind, the back leg is used to put strong pressure on the heelside, as Kristin shows in the photographs. To be able to utilize the forces arising, a high degree of body tension must be built up. To give a more relaxed hold on the *bar* and to be able to apply more weight against the power of the kite to windward, Kristin takes her front

hand off the *bar* and holds it just above the surface of the water. To be able to ride as close to the wind as possible, a kite position between 10 and 11 o'clock or 1 and 2 o'clock is recommended, equivalent to an angle of approximately 45°. In a stronger wind the kite has to be flown lower, to be able to still press the edge into the water.

Key points for mental imaging:
- **Fly kite at roughly 45°**
- **Put strong pressure on the heelside**
- **Keep centre of gravity over the back leg.**

041

The position on the board changes together with how hard the rider edges depending on the prevailing wind conditions.

When riding underpowered, the board is kept flatter on the water. Kristin cannot edge too hard, as otherwise she would lose speed. To power the kite, she pulls the *bar* towards her and flies in a figure eight pattern.

Once the optimum kite pressure has been reached, the board can be edged harder. The posture is relaxed, the arms are loose on the *bar* and the kite can be flown smoothly.

Kristin reacts to an overpowered kite by increasing the edge pressure, twisting her body to windward, assuming a deep kite position and bringing her front arm to the surface of the water.

Tip: Letting your hand slide in the water automatically gives a riding position that makes going upwind easier.

Steering with the board

To be able to go upwind, a rider must be able to go to windward from a reach or broad reach. In the surf, this is not only necessary for getting out when the wind is blowing onshore, but also to be able to cross waves. Furthermore, going to windward is itself an essential prerequisite for all jumps. Bearing away is necessary to change one's direction to leeward, which is also called for when crossing waves, and also for taking speed out of the board, initiating the tack *into switch,* to enjoy downwind sessions, and also to avoid collisions with other kitesurfers.

By putting strong pressure on the rear heelside, Kristin steers her board more into the wind, thus going to windward. She carves upwind, which she initiates by turning her upper body and shifting her centre of gravity towards the centre of the carve. Kiters with experience of snowboarding may remember their backside turn, the turn over the heelside, and visualize the pertinent movement imagery.

042

Key points for mental imaging:
- Press hard on back foot
- Ride on backside edge
- Turn upper body in strongly.

Going to windward

Going to windward.

Riding switch

Bearing away

Bearing away.

Riding *switch* actually means nothing other than riding in a reverse position on the board. The board is held in the water on the toeside, so the upper body must be turned to windward in this riding position. Being able to ride in the *switch stance* opens up a host of options: from this position you can simply jibe into backside riding, a jibe via the toeside can lead into riding in *switch stance,* and following a jump it's possible to land *switch* or you can take off *switch*. This position on the board also opens up a variety of possibilities when riding waves.

Tip: Riding *switch* is much easier if the rider takes his front hand off the *bar.* The rider's body then turns automatically in the riding direction and it's easier to hold course.

Note: The term 'riding *switch*' is not actually correct from a wakeboarding viewpoint. Wakeboarders ride '*toeside*', thus on the toe edge. In wakeboarding, *switch* means 'wrong direction', such as when one lands a trick on one's 'bad' side, for example. However, since *switch* is a more commonly used term among kitesurfers, we will also use it at times in this book.

There are various options for getting into the *switch* stance. The tack into *switch* is described in the turning manoeuvres further below. These are the other two options:

In bearing away, the corresponding snowboarding movement worth remembering is the frontside turn, the turn via the toeside. Kristin puts pressure onto the toeside of her board with her back foot, making a slight carve to leeward by shifting her centre of gravity accordingly and turning her upper body into the centre of the carve.

Key points for mental imaging:
- Put the board flat on the water
- Shift weight to toeside
- Lean upper body into the movement.

Switching the board

The kite is flown in the position between 10 and 11 o'clock or 1 and 2 o'clock throughout the move. To turn her board, Kristin goes upwind, thereby reducing her speed somewhat. Then she shifts her body weight onto the front, right leg, which is put under strong pressure, enabling her to turn her board easily with the back, left leg. As she starts to turn, she shifts her centre of gravity over the centre of the board. At the end of the turn, Kristin edges hard on the toeside to keep her board on course.

When **switching in a small jump**, the kite should be flown at the 11 or 1 o'clock position and must not be moved. The only difference from the board switching illustrated is that this manoeuvre has to be performed at somewhat greater speed, in order to convert it into take-off energy when popping from the surface of the water. The board is turned upon releasing by turning the lower body. Upon landing, the board should be as flat as possible, so as to get pressure onto the toeside of the board by edging accordingly.

Key points for mental imaging:
- Fly kite at roughly 45°
- Go to windward
- Weight onto front leg
- Turn board with back leg
- Weight into centre
- Pressure on toeside and weight back.

Riding blind

'Riding blind' is actually not a basic skill in the classic sense, rather it's one for experts, because landing blind probably demands a lot of the rider's balancing abilities. With regard to the long-term training process, it is advisable to return to this point once you have learned the turning manoeuvres and the first jumps. On the other hand, if you want to increase your balancing ability and your feel for the board substantially at an early stage, you can always try riding in

this manner in lighter winds.

Kristin supports the jump *into blind* by flying her kite in the 11 o'clock position. To take off she brings her centre of gravity well back. As she takes off from the surface of the water, she initiates the rotation from the centre of her body,

takes her back hand off the *bar* and then pulls the board around with her front, left leg. She supports the rotation by pushing away with the back, right leg. The landing is undoubtedly the most difficult phase, and Kristin prepares for this while turning in the air by moving her weight over

what is then the back leg. It's very important in this phase to look back and not in the riding direction. Kristin brings her board flat in the water to a broad reach by centring her centre of gravity on the back, left leg and then immediately puts pressure on the toeside as well.

Key points for mental imaging:
- **Kite to 11 o'clock**
- **Take off and rotate**
- **Release back hand**
- **Weight over back leg**
- **Look backwards**
- **Land via the back leg.**

Turning manoeuvres

Sitting jibe

- **Sitting jibe**
- **Train jibe**
- **Jibe from switch**
- **Jibe into switch**

Together with starting and riding, the turning manoeuvres form the basis for kitesurfing, because ultimately the rider wants to get back to where he started. In this part we only show the simpler turning manoeuvres to start with; aerial turning manoeuvres are introduced once the first jumps have been accomplished successfully.

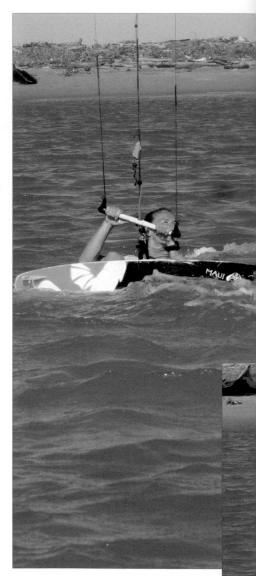

In this first simple turning manoeuvre, the kiter briefly comes to a stop, making it the easiest turning manoeuvre. It should therefore be learned first. The sitting jibe is also the way of changing direction in which least ground is lost.

While going upwind, Kristin flies the kite slowly upwards and brakes by edging the board until she comes to a complete stop. Then she shifts her centre of gravity backwards so that she comes into contact with the water. While steering the kite into the other direction she aligns herself into the new riding direc-

tion and extends her legs so that the kite can pull her up onto the board. As she accelerates on the new course, Kristin puts pressure on the heelside.

Key points for mental imaging:
- Go to windward and kite 12 o'clock
- Sink back into the water
- Push board onto new course
- Steer kite in new riding direction
- Pull up and put pressure on heels.

Train jibe

On some types of trains and trams there is neither a 'front' nor a 'back', they simply change direction. This is how the trick got its name. The critical moment in this turning manoeuvre is the one in which the kite is steered through the zenith: if the pressure upwards is too small, the lift will not be sufficient and the train jibe unintentionally becomes a sitting jibe; if the kite is piloted too quickly through the zenith, the train jibe turns into an aerial transition.

As in the sitting jibe, Kristin steers the kite up while going upwind. At the moment when the kite reaches the zenith, she pushes her board into the new riding direction with what is now the front foot in this direction. She then swings the kite in the new riding direction and shifts her weight onto what is now the back leg and the heelside. The stronger the wind, the less Kristin must bear away initially to pick up speed.

051

Key points for mental imaging:
- Go to windward and kite 12 o'clock
- Slow down and stop
- Pilot kite in new riding direction
- Pressure on heelside.

Jibe from switch

Like the backside turn in snowboarding, this kite manoeuvre basically consists of switching from toeside to heelside. This variation on the jibe is somewhat easier at first than the *into switch*, as it's easier to put pressure on the rear edge than the front. Considerable turn dynamics can be generated in this turning manoeuvre and thus spray can be produced.

Kristin executes the manoeuvre into *switch* with one hand and steers the kite opposite the riding direction towards the 11 o'clock position. This produces considerable tension in the lines. At the moment at which her kite passes through the zenith Kristin transfers the pressure from the toeside to the heelside and, assisted by an upper body turn, enters

the curve. As she does so, she shifts her centre of gravity backwards slightly, and then strongly as she reaches the middle of the curve. The degree of edge pressure and thus the dynamics depend on the speed and the curve radius. In the middle of the curve Kristin also changes hands, which enables her to turn her upper body even more towards the

middle of the curve. By the way, even very confident riders should not perform this manoeuvre ahead of an obstruction to leeward (see Chapter 1 "Safety First"). In this situation, according to Kristin, a sitting tack would be preferable, so please don't copy!

Key points for mental imaging:
- Ride switch
- Steer kite slowly opposite the riding direction
- Change edge
- Weight back
- Lean into curve and carve
- Pressure on heelside.

Jibe into switch

As already described elsewhere, riders who have mastered the frontside turn in snowboarding can quickly learn the jibe *into switch*, as these turning techniques are both introduced by a change from heelside to toeside.

Kristin bears away slightly as she steers the kite into the new riding direction. Once the kite has passed through the zenith into the new direction, she edges on the toeside, brings her centre of gravity back slightly and starts the jibe dynamically by turning her upper body in the direction of the curve. The timing is important here, as she must not start the turn too soon. If she did, she would ride

'underneath' her kite and take the speed out of the carve. At the end of the turn, thus on the new course, Kristin edges the board hard on the toeside and further back, in order to counter the power of the kite to leeward and to maintain ground.

Both in the jibe from *switch stance* and *into switch*, the kite should be steered initially right up through the zenith into the new riding direction. With more experience, the first curve radius can be reduced and then the kite can be flown lower, or kiteloop into the new riding direction, which increases the power of the kite and thus the dynamics of the jibe: the power in the turning motion must be increased, which in turn increases the pressure on the edge and produces stronger spray. The two jibes shown call for good timing when executed into the lip of the wave, which increases the turning sensation considerably.

The crucial factor in carrying out this dynamic manoeuvre successfully is the kite steering, which must match the turning motion exactly in time.

Key points for mental imaging:
- Kite at 1 or 11 o'clock
- Change to toeside
- Lie into the turn, pressure on back leg
- Carve
- Straighten up and continue to put pressure on toeside.

Airtime

Man has long cherished the dream of flying, and has been able to fulfil this dream in many respects. In kite surfing, however, flying assumes another dimension: due to the height, but also due to the many variations on athleticism, it's an experience that is hard to beat and which can always provide a gratifying rush of adrenaline.

Once a rider has mastered the board and no longer has problems with kite steering, he has finally reached the point of discovering what this sport is really all about: airtime. Taking off and floating over the sea for a few seconds, and then landing smoothly again is an unbelievable feeling that has considerable potential to become addictive. It is not without justification that the French call our sport 'flysurfing'. But a word of caution: the trial

- **From chop hop to board off**
- **Rotation jumps**
- **Aerial turning manoeuvres**
- **Unhooked Jumps**
- **Kiteloops**
- **Handlepasses**

and error method of learning has proved particularly painful when learning the first jumps, especially rotation jumps. Many injuries, in particular bruised and broken ribs, are caused by unsuccessful rotation jumps. It would be the right time here to add a reminder here about learning to use the mental imaging method, which has proved helpful in extreme sports activities (the injury ratio of 7 per 1000 hours of activity puts kitesurfing into this category; see Chapter 1 "Safety first"), and reduces the risk of injury.

Before practising the first jump, the **take-off** should be clarified here as a basic element of all jumps. The perfect **timing** of the following components has proved crucial:

- The power of the kite, caused by its position or its movement;
- The take-off momentum;
- Going upwind and edging extremely hard;
- When taking off via a wave, the timing must be matched to the wave.

If the timing of all these elements is coordinated satisfactorily, then the jump will be successful. The course steered and the position of the kite can strongly influence one or more components and are decisive for the success of the jump.

As the illustration shows, the edge of the wind window moves further backwards as the speed increases. This has consequences for the take-off; very experienced kiters pick up high speed, due to which the kite flies deeper into the wind window on account of the changed angle of the apparent wind. They then cut quickly into the wind by edging hard on the heelside. The kite flies less quickly back in the windward direction, so that a very strong pull is generated on the lines. This energy is converted together with a powerful take-off momentum into height. For less practised riders, the danger here naturally consists in not achieving a clean take-off. This mostly happens when the

Figure 5: How the edge of the wind window changes when taking off at increased speed on a reach.

kiter is going too fast, or releases the edge too early and is not edging hard and long enough upwind to get the right take-off. And edging is crucial to the success of a jump. To progressively develop a clean take-off, we recommend trying the first jumps at slow speed from a close reach. The speed should then be increased gradually, which will bringing the kite more into the softzone and thus

increase the pull on the lines. The rider can slowly increase the degree of edging in this way and learn to control it. It is only in this way that a perfectly timed take-off can be achieved, to be rewarded with height, safety and a clean landing.

From Chop hop to board off

The introduction and ascent to greater heights via the *chop hop* has proved its worth, as this first jump is the best way to gain experience on which to build for all further jumps. Taking off without the support of the kite and without the aid of a take-off ramp in the form of a wave is the best exercise for gaining height in all other jumps.

- Chop hop
- Jump with kite steering
- Jump into switch
- Jump from toeside
- Tailgrab
- One footer
- Board off

Chop hop

Kristin flies her kite in a fixed position at roughly 11 o'clock throughout the jump. To start with, a high kite position just a little below the zenith is advisable. She approaches the jump on a reach. Then she goes to windward, shifts her centre of gravity back, puts strong pressure on the heelside and thus gets maximum tension in the lines. To take off, she flexes her knees and in this way creates tension that is then released into a powerful take-off. Kristin releases strongly from the back leg and while in the air she pulls the board up underneath her body. To land, she extends her legs again, absorbing the landing by flexing her knees.

Key points for mental imaging:
- Kite at 11 o'clock
- Go to windward
- Flex knees and take off powerfully
- Pull board up underneath body
- Extend legs
- Land.

Jump with kite steering

A normal jump with kite steering forms the basis for many of the other jumps and should therefore be practised in both directions until it has been properly mastered.

Kristin approaches the jump on a reach and at moderate speed. Before the take-off she steers her kite back opposite her riding direction to at least 12 o'clock and goes upwind as she does this, moving her centre of gravity to the back leg, in this case the right leg. By doing this, she builds up the pressure required to take off. Steering the kite back towards the 12 to 1 o'clock position causes it to generate vertical energy that Kristin counters by edging hard, thereby increasing the pull on the lines further. In addition, she pulls her *bar* towards her, powering the kite in this way and further increasing the take-off energy. Now she triggers the upward movement by exerting dynamic pressure via the board edge. The decisive momentum here is the edge pressure; if this is relinquished too soon, the jump ends with a swinging movement below

the kite and with a crash into the water. After releasing into the jump, Kristin bends her legs to get her centre of gravity as close to the *bar* as possible and thus avoid excessive swinging. She continues to pull the *bar* actively towards her, to increase the lift. She maintains this position throughout the flight phase. After she has passed the highest point of her jump, she begins to steer the kite forward towards the 11 o'clock position slowly, in order to prepare for a soft landing and to be able to ride away with enough speed. Just before landing, Kristin extends her legs so that she can then absorb the landing using her knees.

Key points for mental imaging:
- **Steer kite towards 12 o'clock and go to windward**
- **Hold edge and pull bar towards you**
- **When kite is at 12 to 12:30, release edge and jump off forcefully**
- **Bend legs and hold kite in the zenith**
- **Steer kite lightly into riding direction and land.**

060

Jump into switch

This trick differs from a normal jump in the landing and thus also in the final phase of flying: prior to take-off, Kristin steers the kite up from a 45° position into at least the 12 o'clock position and cuts upwind as she does so, shifting her centre of gravity to the rear, left leg. The

increased pull on the lines enables her to generate the required energy for the take-off. In addition, she pulls the *bar* towards her, which powers the kite and further increases the energy. By pushing down hard with the rear, left leg, she lifts off from the water. She continues to pull the *bar* actively towards her, to increase the lift. After passing the highest point of the jump, she begins to steer her kite forwards gradually in the direction of the

1 o'clock position, to get sufficient tension in the lines, which keeps her from underlying the kite. Well before landing on a broad reach to running, Kristin turns the board clockwise via the lee side to *switch*. She lands her board with the toeside to windward, softening her knees as she does so. Upon landing, she immediately edges on the toeside and puts pressure on the rear, right leg.

Key points for mental imaging:
• Steer kite towards 12 o'clock and go to windward
• Hold edge and power bar
• When kite across zenith, release edge and jump off energetically
• Turn board to switch
• Steer kite in riding direction and land.

Jump from toeside

The difficulty about this trick is that the take-off movement is performed from an unfamiliar position in which it's harder to build up the necessary pressure from the toeside.

Kristin rides toeside with the kite in the 1 o'clock position, goes upwind and as she does so steers the kite back towards the zenith. The pull on the lines is thus increased. Once enough energy has been generated for the take-off, she releases powerfully via the back leg. In the flight phase she turns the board counter-clockwise back into the normal position. When she has passed the highest point of the jump, she steers the kite forwards in the riding direction and cushions the landing with her knees.

Key points for mental imaging:
- Ride toeside
- Steer kite towards 12 o'clock and go to windward
- Once kite across zenith, release edge and take off over back leg
- Turn board back
- Steer kite in riding direction and land.

Tail grab

The *tail grab* is the easiest grab trick to learn, as shifting the centre of gravity backwards and at the same time pulling on the board tail in the flight phase do not disrupt the natural sequence of the jump and only complicate it to a small extent. Furthermore, the *grab* should be regarded as a prerequisite for the *one foot* jump and should be practised accordingly before performing this jump. When grabbing the board with one hand it helps to keep the other hand in the middle of the *bar* so as not to mis-steer the kite.

Kristin takes off as in a simple high jump, but shortly after the take-off she leans far back and grabs the edge of her board with the rear hand. Then she pulls her board towards her, bending her back leg at the same time. On the descent, Kristin releases her hand from the board and returns it to the *bar* for better control, initiating the landing by steering her kite forwards.

Key points for mental imaging:
• Kite at 11 or 1 o'clock and go to windward
• Kite towards 12 o'clock and hold edge
• Release edge and take off powerfully
• Weight to rear and grab edge, hold kite in zenith
• Hand on bar
• Steer kite in riding direction and land.

One footer

Once the tail grab has been mastered, it's time to go a stage further. At this point the rear hand no longer just comes into contact with the board but holds it actively, so that the rear foot can be taken out of the strap and extended away from the board.

Kristin takes off as in a normal jump and then proceeds as for the tail grab. As she grabs her board securely by the tail – upper body and board are moving towards one another – she slips her back foot out of its strap and extends her leg as far away as possible from the board. In the approach to landing, she returns her foot to the strap, holding the grab and steering the kite forwards. It is advisable to keep an eye on the strap in this manoeuvre, so as to be able to return the foot directly to it. Shortly before

landing she releases her board, spots the landing and prepares to land on a down-wind reach. Kristin only returns her rear

hand to the *bar* here after landing, but she could quite easily do this earlier for better control.

Both in the *one foot* and the *board off* manoeuvres, it's important to avoid landing with just one foot in the strap, as the risk of twisting the knee or ankle due to an adverse lever action would be very high. Even Kristin, when working on performing the jumps illustrated, always preferred to kick the board off completely and land without it if she couldn't get her foot back into the strap before landing.

Key points for mental imaging:
- **Kite at 11 or 1 o'clock and go to windward**
- **Kite towards 12 o'clock and edge**
- **Release edge and take off energetically**
- **Weight back, grab edge and take rear foot out of strap**
- **Foot into strap and kite towards 11 or 1 o'clock**
- **Land.**

Board off

As she heads upwind prior to take-off, Kristin grabs the *bar* in the centre with her front, left hand to avoid executing any accidental steering movements. Then she jumps off hard, bringing her legs and board up as high as possible. Here, too, upper body and board move towards one another. Kristin grabs her board on the toeside between the two straps. She pulls the board from her feet, holds it in her outstretched arm and extends her legs horizontally while hanging onto the *bar*. After a short flight phase in this position, she steers her kite forward a little towards the 11 o'clock position, flexes her legs and puts the board back onto her feet. To land on a broad reach she puts both hands back on the *bar* and controls the landing.

Key points for mental imaging:
- Hold *bar* in the middle and go to windward
- Steer kite high, release edge and jump off energetically
- Keep weight over board and pull knees up
- Grab board and remove from feet
- Extend legs
- Pull feet up to body and insert into straps
- Steer kite in riding direction
- Land.

Tips:
1. Extended hangtime is required for this trick.
2. The first *board off* tricks can be learnt more easily with a handle on the board, as it can be reached and controlled better in this way.

Rotation jumps

- Backflip without kite steering
- Backflip with kite steering
- Frontflip without kite steering
- Frontflip with kite steering
- Front with tailgrab
- One foot 360°
- Double back grabbed

Experience shows that the backflip is the easiest rotation jump to learn and should accordingly be practised first. As demonstrated in other sections, this jump depends particularly on the rider's orientation capacity. He must be aware of the position of his own body in space, together with the position of the kite and the forces arising from it that act on the body. Often the rotation is performed too energetically in the initial 'flip' attempts and the jump is 'over-rotated', which can result in some hard landings on one's back. The same thing can happen if the rotation is launched too slowly. Being aware of the kite in the air without looking at it is important and can be practised with the aid of suitable exercises (see Chapter 5 "Specific warm-up") just like general orientation ability can.

Because the backflip can easily be done with or without steering the kite, this trick should be practised as a basis for all other rotation manoeuvres. A powerful take-off over a small wind wave can also help.

Backflip without kite steering

Kristin performs this rotation jump with the kite fixed roughly in the 11 o'clock position. She holds the *bar* in the middle to avoid any steering movements during the rotation. She goes hard to windward before taking off and pulls the *bar* towards her, thereby increasing the tension in the lines. She lays her upper body back, creating a lever effect, which helps to get the board out of the water. The strong take-off push by the back leg is combined with a rotation impulse from the middle of the body, which is aided by turning the head in the direction of rotation. To prevent over-rotating, the rotation must be carefully regulated during the continued flight phase by extending or flexing the legs. In this sequence, the legs are flexed slightly in the flight phase; Kristin only extends them fully again at the end, thus stopping the rotation and preparing to land on a broad reach.

Key points for mental imaging:
- Kite at 11 or 1 o'clock
- Go to windward and power the kite
- Take off over back leg and begin to turn
- Turn head
- Extend legs
- Land.

073

Backflip with kite steering

Kristin steers the kite back from the 1 o'clock position to the 12 o'clock position and cuts upwind. At the moment at which the pull on the lines gets stronger, she takes off powerfully from her back leg and thus from the *tail* of her board. As she pushes off, Kristin starts to rotate immediately with the aid of suitable momentum, which is supported by turning her head in the direction of rotation; she throws her head back. During the flight phase, her legs are flexed slightly; following a ¾-turn, when the surface of the water is sighted once again, Kristin extends her legs in preparation for landing and to break the rotation. At the same time she steers the kite forward into the 1 o'clock position, so as to be able to ride away upon landing. The landing on the water should be absorbed well by the knees.

Key points for mental imaging:
- Kite at 1 or 11 o'clock
- Kite back to 12 o'clock
- Take off and start rotation
- Head back and flex legs
- Extend legs, pull front hand
- Land.

Frontflip without

Kristin performs this frontflip with the kite in a fixed position at roughly 1 o'clock. To avoid steering movements, she holds the *bar* in the centre. Before taking off she turns sharply to windward and pulls the *bar* towards her, increasing the pull on the lines. At the same time as she takes off from the back leg, she starts the

forward rotation from the middle of her body, aiding the rotation momentum by moving her head in the same direction. During the rotation Kristin's legs are slightly flexed; she only extends them fully again at the end, thereby stopping the rotation and preparing to land on a broad reach.

Key points for mental imaging:
- **Kite at 1 or 11 o'clock**
- **Go to windward**
- **Pop and start forward rotation**
- **Flex legs**
- **Extend legs**
- **Land.**

kite steering

Frontflip with kite

Approaching on a reach, Kristin flies her kite in the 11 o'clock position. She cuts into the wind and steers her kite towards 12 o'clock, to get strong tension in the lines. She holds the edge until she has built up enough energy to release and takes off via her back, right leg. She now shifts her centre of gravity slightly in the direction of the forward rotation. During the first flight phase she then increases the rotation momentum forwards and pulls the board up towards her by bending her legs. After ¾ of the rotation, Kristin begins to extend her legs, thereby stopping the rotation, and starts to steer her kite forwards towards the 11 o'clock position. She bends her knees to absorb the landing on a broad reach.

steering

Key points for mental imaging:
- Kite at 11 or 1 o'clock
- Go to windward and kite high towards zenith
- Take off and start rotating forwards
- Draw board towards body
- Extend legs and kite forwards
- Land.

General tip on rotation jumps: With your legs bent, it's possible to rotate quickly due to the fact that legs and board are closer to the pivot point, whereas you rotate more slowly when the legs aren't flexed quite so much. This is a way of adjusting the speed of rotation.

Front with tail grab

Kristin cuts sharply into the wind and steers her kite towards 12 o'clock. She holds the edge until she has built up enough energy for the take-off and releases the back leg. She shifts her centre of gravity slightly in the direction of the rotation that now follows, i.e. forwards. During the initial flight phase she increases the rotation momentum forwards and supports this by turning her head in the direction of rotation. She takes her back hand from the bar and grabs the tail of the board. This is the optimum position for this jump and at the same time a preliminary exercise for

the *one foot 360°*, which follows later. After ¾ of the rotation, Kristin releases the *grab* and begins to extend her legs, ending the rotation. She steers her kite forwards towards the 11 o'clock position and lands on a broad reach, absorbing the landing with her knees.

Key points for mental imaging:
- Kite at 11 o'clock
- Edge hard and kite high towards zenith
- Take off and start forward rotation
- Grab edge
- Release edge and extend legs
- Kite in riding direction and land.

One foot 360°

A good hangtime is required for this trick, so Kristin has to be particularly dynamic in her take-off and needs to steer the kite back fast and aggressively. She flies her kite on a reach at the 11 o'clock position, edges upwind and then steers her kite towards 12 o'clock to get tension in the lines. She then jumps off using the back, right leg. Immediately on take-off she brings her centre of gravity forwards and starts to rotate straight away. She flexes her legs to bring the board close to her body, takes her rear hand off the *bar* and grabs the rear edge of the board. Once she has a firm hold on the board, she can take her rear foot out of the strap and then extend it away from the board. After ¾ of the rotation, she pulls the board back onto her rear foot, moving foot and board towards one another as she does so, and begins to land. She brings the kite forward and pulls herself back into position over the board. She cushions the landing on a broad reach with her knees.

Key points for mental imaging:
- Edge upwind and steer kite up
- Take off and start rotating forwards
- Bring board and hand together and grab rear edge
- Back foot out of strap and extend
- Keep head in direction of rotation and finish rotation
- Put foot back into strap, release edge
- Hand onto bar, extend legs, kite forwards
- Land.

Tip: To maintain the rotation, the rider should keep looking over his shoulder throughout the trick. It's therefore necessary to get the foot into the strap without looking.

Double back grabbed

The double turn backwards is performed in exactly the same way as the single backflip, although more time is required for two turns, so Kristin supports this jump by steering her kite. Prior to take-off she edges upwind and steers the kite from the 1 to 2 o'clock position back to the 12 o'clock position. The increased tension in the lines gives her the required take-off energy, which she amplifies further by pushing off powerfully with the back leg. Kristin begins to turn from the centre of her body even as she takes off. As she rotates, she takes her rear hand off the *bar*. By flexing her legs she uses her centre of gravity to get closer to her board, making it easier to rotate fast. During the second turn she starts to steer her kite forwards, thus commencing the landing. She only puts her hand back onto the *bar* at the end of the second turn and extends her legs, although not fully, shortly before landing.

Key points for mental imaging:
- Edge upwind and pull kite up to 12 o'clock
- Take off over back leg
- Start rotation on take-off
- Rear hand to heelside and flex knees fully
- Maintain position for up to 1½ turns and focus on landing area
- Steer kite forwards and extend legs
- Land.

Aerial turning manoeuvres build on normal jumps and are an elegant way of turning the board to the new riding direction. As with normal jumps, however, their height should be increased slowly.

- Aerial transition
- Backflip transition
- Frontflip transition

Aerial turning manoeuvres

Aerial transition

On the approach to the aerial transition, also known as a *transition jump*, Kristin is already flying the kite very high. To take off she edges hard to windward. She then steers her kite towards the 12 o'clock position until she feels a powerful pull on the lines, and when this moment is reached she takes off. At the highest point of the jump, she points herself and her board in the new riding direction and steers her kite further in this new direction. This must happen at the right time, as otherwise the kite would lack power and the manoeuvre would end 'in the water'. As with all landings, Kristin flexes her knees to absorb the landing. On the new course, she puts pressure on the back leg.

Key points for mental imaging:
- Kite back slightly to 12 o'clock and go to windward
- Take off over back leg
- Align into new riding direction
- Kite forwards
- Land.

087

BACK- AND FRONTFLIP TRANSITION

The normal rotation jumps have to be mastered first as a prerequisite for this type of turning manoeuvre. The crucial difference is the kite steering; to be able to influence this directly during a rotation, it's imperative to retain one's orientation throughout the jump. This means in turn that the kiter has to know the position his body assumes in the air in each phase of the rotation and which position the kite is in.

Kristin slows her speed by edging windward and steering the kite high. She steers her kite to the 12 o'clock position, increasing the pull on the lines. On take-off Kristin starts to rotate immediately. During the turn she flexes her legs,

Backflip transition

extending them again to terminate the rotation. At the same time, she steers her kite in the new riding direction at the end of the turn to regain the line tension and be able to ride away. She aligns into the new riding direction and cushions the landing with her knees.

Key points for mental imaging:
- **Edge and kite to 12 o'clock**
- **Take off and start rotating**
- **Flex knees**
- **Steer kite in new direction**
- **Extend legs, align**
- **Land.**

Tip: At the moment that the kite develops the strongest pull when steered into the zenith, the rider can virtually hang on the kite and turn. For easier orientation it also makes sense to take the front hand off the bar and grip the bar in the centre with the back hand. The kite is automatically steered in the right direction this way and the landing can be controlled satisfactorily.

Frontflip transition

To reduce her speed, Kristin edges hard to windward and steers the kite to the 12 o'clock position, thereby increasing the tension in the lines. As she takes off, Kristin starts the forward rotation from the middle of her body and supports this momentum by moving her head in the same direction. During the rotation she flexes her legs, extending them again to end the rotation. At the same time, she steers her kite gently throughout the turn and more strongly towards the end into the new riding direction, to regain the line tension and to be able to ride away.

She absorbs the landing with her knees.
Once the two 360° transition jumps have been securely mastered, more rotations can be added if desired.

Key points for mental imaging:
- Go to windward and steer kite back to 12 o'clock
- Take off and start rotation
- Flex knees
- Steer kite further towards 2 or 10 o'clock
- Extend knees
- Land.

Unhooked jumps are derived from wakeboarding, in which there is no harness hook. They are performed with the kite in a fixed position at between 10 and 11 or 2 and 1 o'clock, and so, wakeboard-like, are lower altitude jumps. Before taking off it's advisable to pull in the adjuster and depower the kite, so that the kite is controllable when unhooked and does not develop too much pull. All *unhooked* jumps are distinguished accordingly by *power* and naturally give rise to high forces, which act on the shoulders for the most part; thus it's worth referring again at this point to the strengthening of the shoulder rotator muscles and pectoral girdle muscles (see Chapter 9 "Training ashore") required to prevent anything, especially an injury, from spoiling the fun to be had with these tricks. For these jumps it's also advisable not to go too hard to windward initially, and to practise them from a reach or broad reach position.

Unhooked jumps

- **Unhooking**
- **Hooking in**
- **Railey to revert**
- **Unhooked back**
- **Unhooked front**
- **Indy glide**
- **Indy front**

Unhooking

Prior to unhooking, the adjuster should be pulled in to depower the kite. To do this, the kite set-up must be right, i.e. the kite should be adjusted correctly; this means that it mustn't be powered too much and shouldn't 'deform' if the *bar* is pulled all the way in, although the back lines mustn't sag too much either, so that the kite can still be steered. To be able to unhook easily, the pressure on the kite has then to be reduced somewhat, which can be achieved by bearing away slightly. Kristin unhooks the chickenloop with a tug on the *bar*.

Tip: When unhooking Kristin uses her thumbs to help press the chickenloop out of the harness hook. This is particularly helpful with a curved harness hook.

Hooking in

To reduce the pressure on the kite when hooking in again, the same applies as when unhooking: bear away. The hooking-in itself can be done in two ways. It is possible to leave both hands on the *bar* and to hook back in again by pulling the *bar* towards the hook. The thumbs can be used again here for assistance, to help press the loop into the harness hook. The other possibility, which Kristin demonstrates here, is to take one hand off the *bar* and hook the chickenloop into the hook using this hand, depowering the kite at the same time.

094

Railey

When looking at this trick it becomes clear how useful it can be to be able to wakeboard. The *railey* is performed without kite steering and is also a relatively low altitude trick, so there's nothing to get in the way of the true wakeboard style.

Kristin flies her kite at the 10 o'clock position and picks up maximum speed on a reach. To obtain strong line tension and thus generate energy for the take-off, she edges hard, presses her board into the water with the back leg and builds up as much pressure as possible. Then she

releases the edge abruptly, and as a result the kite literally tears her out of the water. As she takes off Kristin goes into a full body stretch and brings the board above head height. In the air she follows the pull of the lines. She pulls herself closer to the *bar* again as if doing pull-ups and pulls the board under her body in preparation for landing. To absorb the landing, it should be approached on a broad reach and of course the landing should be cushioned well using the knees.

Key points for mental imaging:
• Kite at 45° and unhook
• Build up strong pressure and take off
• Extend body and let the kite pull you
• Pull actively towards the bar and bring board under the body
• Absorb landing with the knees.

Railey to revert

This jump is a *railey* with a landing on the *toeside*.

The phases of the jump up to the point at which the landing is commenced are therefore the same. As Kristin pulls the board under her body, she turns it clockwise onto the toeside and lands.

After landing on a broad reach, she edges on the toeside and continues to ride toeside.

Key points for mental imaging:
- 1 or 11 o'clock
- Unhook and hands to middle
- Extend body
- Pull actively towards the bar
- Turn board to toeside
- Land.

Unhooked back

Kristin holds her *bar* in the middle and flies the kite in the 1 o'clock position. To take off she edges to windward, pushing off from the back, left leg immediately starting the backward rotation using momentum from the middle of her body. During the rotation her body axis is briefly horizontal, as the kite pulls her forcefully horizontally. To accelerate the rotation, she pulls herself towards the *bar* and flexes her legs slightly. At the end of the rotation, she extends her legs again and lands on a broad reach, absorbing the landing with her knees.

Key points for mental imaging:
• **Grip bar in the middle and unhook**
• **Kite at 1 or 11 o'clock and edge upwind**
• **Take off and start backward rotation**
• **Bend knees and arms**
• **Straighten out after ¾-turn**
• **Land.**

Unhooked front

After unhooking, Kristin holds the *bar* in the centre. With her kite in a position between I and 2 o'clock, she cuts hard to windward to take off. On take-off using the rear, left leg, she begins the rotation using suitable momentum from the middle of her body, assisted by corresponding movement of the head. Kristin speeds up the rotation by pulling on the *bar* and bending her legs. At the end of the rotation, she extends her legs again, pulls herself over her board and lands the jump on a broad reach, absorbing the landing with her knees.

Key points for mental imaging:
- Kite at 1:30 or 10:30 and go to windward
- Unhook and hands in centre
- Take off and rotate forwards
- After ¾-turn, extend legs
- Pull board underneath body
- Land.

Indy glide

To avoid any steering movements, Kristin holds her *bar* in the middle. She flies her kite to the 11 o'clock position, going hard to windward as she does so. Once the maximum line tension is reached, she takes off powerfully against the resistance of the water by extending her back leg impulsively. She immediately takes her back hand off the *bar* to grab the toeside of her board with it, aiding this manoeuvre by bending her knees. The strong pull of the kite on one arm in the 11 o'clock position results almost automatically in the downward position of the board that is typical of this trick. As she turns the board back in the riding direction, Kristin maintains the grab, only taking her hand off the edge and returning it to the *bar* shortly before landing.

Key points for mental imaging:
- Kite 11 or 1 o'clock and turn to windward
- Powerful take-off and release rear hand
- Bend knees, back hand grabs toeside of board
- Hold edge and be pulled by kite
- Hand onto bar and land.

Tip: It is recommended that with all single-handed *unhooked* jumps, you grip the *bar* right in the centre with the hand that remains on the *bar.* In this case the depower line is located either between the middle finger and the ring finger or between the index finger and the middle finger.

Indy front

For this trick too Kristin holds the *bar* in the centre and unhooks. She flies the kite in the 11 o'clock position and goes upwind to take off. As she takes off over the back, right leg she has already released her back hand from the *bar* and starts the forward rotation. Due to the strong horizontal pull of the kite, Kristin is pulled virtually behind it during the rotation. Her left arm is extended and she pulls the board towards her to grab the toeside edge between the straps with her right hand. She holds this position for as long as possible, only releasing the grab and extending her legs again shortly before landing. She lands on a broad reach, absorbing the landing with her knees. After landing, she grips the *bar* with both hands once again and edges on the heelside.

Key points for mental imaging:
- Unhook, hands to middle and kite at 11 or 1 o'clock
- Edge hard and take off
- Release right hand and rotate forwards
- Grab toeside in the middle with the right hand
- After rotating release grip on the edge and extend legs
- Land.

Kiteloops

- **Kiteloop while riding**
- **Hooked-in kiteloop**
- **Hooked-in double back with kiteloop**
- **Unhooked kiteloop**
- **F16**
- **Unhooked downloop**
- **Unhooked downloop s-bend**
- **Kiteloop to blind**

Kiteloops add power and pull to any jump, as the kite is looped through the power zone, accelerating the kiter hard to leeward in the air. If the kite is looped backwards, it's a kiteloop, while a *downloop* is when the kite is looped forwards. The first attempts at a kiteloop should be made when riding and without leaving the water and should then be combined with small jumps in which the board is edged only very slightly, so that unsuccessful landings have less serious consequences. Once these can be managed perfectly, the height of the jump can be increased before rotations are added in. Only then should *unhooked* kiteloops be included in the training programme. In addition to recommending overall muscle strengthening, especially of the hip and leg muscles, we advise you here to wear an impact vest due to the possible increase in speed on impact with the surface of the water.

Kiteloop while riding

Looping the kite while riding is a preliminary exercise for jumps with a kiteloop. The effect is in getting used to the change in pressure and getting a feel for how much pull has to be exerted on the *bar* to get the kite to fly in the loop. Furthermore, different radiuses should be tried out in this exercise, as these will cause different acceleration to leeward depending on the size of the radius.

Kristin flies the kite at the 11 o'clock position. To take the pressure out of the lines, she bears away slightly, steering the kite firmly back through the zenith with her rear hand. She rides a course that guarantees that the kite retains enough pressure for it to be steered. The pull increases as the kite 'plunges' into the power zone, resulting in strong acceleration to leeward. Kristin continues on a reach to a broad reach and edges on the heelside only at the end of the loop.

Key points for mental imaging:
- Kite at 11 or 1 o'clock
- Bear away
- Pull bar back aggressively
- Loop the kite backwards
- Edge on heelside at the end of the kiteloop.

Kristin approaches this jump with the kite at the 11 o'clock position. Prior to take-off, she edges slightly, steers the kite back to the zenith and takes off aggressively over the back leg. As in a normal jump with kite support, she steers the kite further back. Instead of steering the kite slowly forwards at the highest part of the jump, she lets her kite plunge into the power zone by giving a hard tug on the back side of the bar. The kite flies in a loop opposite the riding direction. It is important to maintain this position, in spite of the powerful pull to leeward, until the kite climbs towards the zenith once more and thus loses power. The accelerated landing to leeward must be well cushioned by the knees.

Key points for mental imaging:
- **Kite at 11 or 1 o'clock**
- **Edge and take off**
- **Steer kite back towards 1 or 11 o'clock**
- **Continue to loop kite backwards**
- **Cushion landing with knees.**

Tip: The front hand can be taken off the *bar* to prevent countersteering. With big kites it is also possible to hold onto the back side of the bar with both hands to be able to exert more pressure, causing the kite to loop more quickly.

Hooked-in

kiteloop

Hooked-in double back with kiteloop

This is the most common combined hooked-in kiteloop. Once the rider has got the hang of looping the kite, the *double back* with kiteloop is easy to learn, because once the rider has started to rotate, the second rotation, aided by the looping kite, happens virtually on its own.

The backward rotation is performed simultaneously with the kiteloop. Kristin flies her kite to the 12 o'clock position. She then triggers the kiteloop by strongly steering with the rear hand. Now she only needs to edge to windward in parallel with this and provide momentum for the turn from the middle of her body; she assists this by moving her head. While maintaining the extreme steering motion and continuing to loop the kite, Kristin completes the first back rotation and then experiences strong horizontal acceleration due to the kite flying through the power zone. This also automatically accelerates the rotational movement. She ends the second rotation by

simply yielding to the pull. Kristin continues to pull hard on the right-hand side of the *bar*, due to which the kite moves towards the zenith before the landing. To break off the rotation she now stretches her legs out again. By landing on a broad reach to running, she takes some of the power out of the kite, nevertheless landing at a higher speed due to the acceleration to leeward and absorbing this with her knees.

Key points for mental imaging:
- Go to windward and pull kite back towards 11 or 1 o'clock
- Enter backward rotation with the pull of the kite
- Continue to loop kite backwards and carry on rotating
- Still looping kite backwards, after nearly two turns stretch legs
- Land.

Unhooked kiteloop

This jump should only be included in the training programme when you've mastered both *hooked-in* kiteloops and *unhooked* jumps and they no longer cause a problem. When first attempting the unhooked kiteloop, it is advisable to perform it somewhat underpowered, to slowly get used to the pull to leeward. Some effort is required to master the one-sided hold on the bar, which triggers and maintains the all-out looping of the kite.

In preparation for the kiteloop, Kristin flies her kite to the 12 o'clock position. She bears away slightly and holds the *bar* right on the outside with her right hand, which helps with steering the kite upwards and is very useful during the trick as a whole. Then everything happens very fast: Kristin unhooks and the moment the kite is above her she grabs onto the right-hand side of the *bar* with her left hand also. This starts the kiteloop. With the ensuing pull of the kite she

goes hard to windward and pops from the back leg. Unlike the *railey*, the kite pulls her hard *downwind*. Kristin follows the kite and does not try to resist it. As the kite comes to the end of its loop, she begins to land by bringing the board back under her body. She turns the board onto a broad reach and lands. Landings like this must be cushioned especially well using the knees. Kristin places her left, leading hand back on the forward *bar* side as soon as possible to interrupt the looping of the kite and to control it.

114

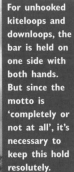

For unhooked kiteloops and downloops, the bar is held on one side with both hands. But since the motto is 'completely or not at all', it's necessary to keep this hold resolutely.

Key points for mental imaging:
- Kite at 12 o'clock
- Bear away slightly and unhook
- Move left hand to back bar side and go to windward
- Take off from back leg as soon as kite develops power
- Continue to loop kite and follow its pull
- When kiteloop is complete, pull board under body and land.

Tip: To slow the looping movement to some extent on small, particularly fast kites, the *bar* can also be held in the middle with the front hand. Some people find it more comfortable to hold the *bar* in the 'fishing rod' position, as Kristin demonstrates in the picture to the left, while others simply place their hands adjacent to one another. In all cases the back part of the *bar*, or the front part for downloops, must be grasped quickly and immediately following unhooking (kite at 12 o'clock).

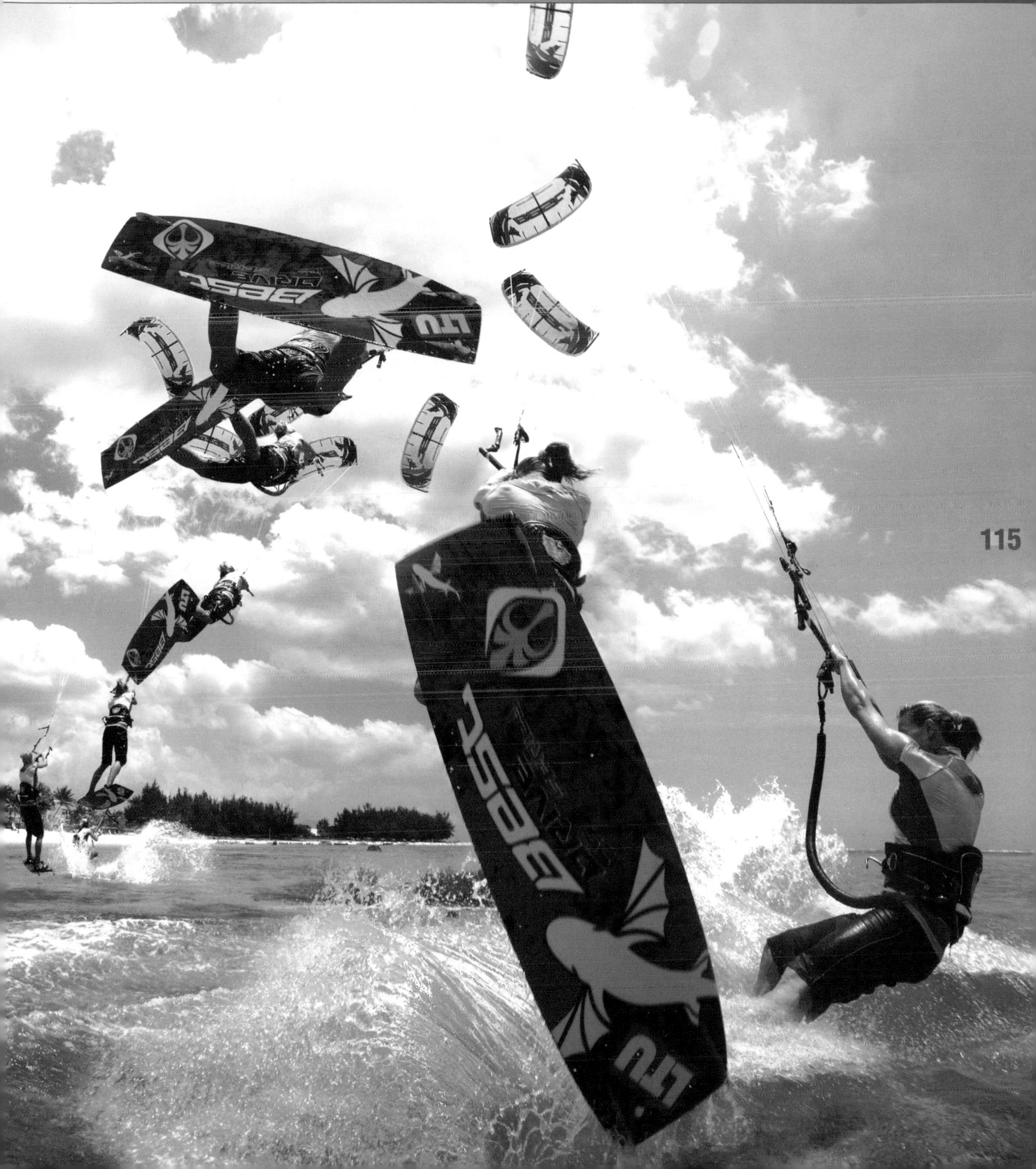
LTU
BEST

F16

The F16 is the most popular *unhooked* kiteloop with rotation. Once you've mastered the *unhooked* kiteloop, you can practise performing a simultaneous rotation. In this trick too, Kristin flies her kite to the 12 o'clock position and bears away slightly. She quickly grips the back part of the bar with both hands, causing the kite to start looping. At the same time, Kristin goes hard to windward and takes off at the moment when the line tension increases. She goes straight into a backward rotation, aided by going upwind. The looping kite pulls Kristin horizontally and *downwind* through the air. She yields to this pull in the rotation by stretching out her body. Once the rotation is complete and at the end of the kiteloop she lands with her knees on a broad reach, to cushion the landing effectively.

Key points for mental imaging:
- Kite to 12 o'clock
- Unhook and grasp back
- As soon as kite gains power, go to windward and start rotating
- Rotate and let the kite pull you
- When kiteloop and rotation are complete, pull board under body and land downwind.

116

To start with, Kristin bears away a little. This makes it easier for her to unhook due to the reduced tension in the lines, and she holds the bar in the centre. Then she flies the kite in the 12 o'clock position and she grabs onto the left-hand side of the bar from underneath with her back, right hand, triggering the downloop. She goes hard upwind, thereby increasing the pull on the lines, which is strengthened still further by the kite 'plunging' downwards. With maximum line tension she takes off powerfully from the back leg. During the flight phase, Kristin continues to pull on the front side of the *bar*, so that the kite can finish its loop. To land she pulls the board back underneath her body and places her right hand back on the right-hand side of the *bar*, ending the looping momentum of the kite. By landing on a broad reach, Kristin takes the power out of the kite and absorbs the landing with her knees.

118

Key points for mental imaging:
- Bear away and unhook
- Go to windward and move back hand to front side of the bar
- Steer kite hard forwards and take off from back leg
- Keep pulling on the bar
- Pull board under body and land.

Unhooked downloop

Kristin flies the kite at 12 o'clock, unhooks and puts her back hand on the front of the *bar*. The kite begins to loop forwards and Kristin goes hard to windward at the same time, thus increasing the pull on the lines and building up energy for a strong take-off. She takes off from the back leg and immediately starts rotating from the middle of her body, moving her head in the same direction. Due to the strong pull of the kite she is pulled behind it, automatically causing her to stretch her body with her arms extended. The greater the radius of the looping kite, bringing it closer to the surface of the water, the more her body is pulled horizontally. After rotating Kristin pulls the board back under her body again and approaches the landing on a broad reach or running, absorbing the landing with her knees.

Key points for mental imaging:
- Bear away and unhook
- Grip the front side of the bar with the back hand too and turn to windward
- Steer kite strongly forwards and take off from back leg
- Start forward rotation
- Pull board under body and land.

Unhooked downloop s-bend

Kiteloop to blind

Kiteloops and downloops can also be combined with many other tricks. Further rotations can be added, for example, and handlepasses included. Kiteloop handlepasses in every conceivable variation are very popular with the pros, but copying is not recommended due to the very high forces generated and the risk of injury associated with these. Nevertheless, Kristin shows us here the simplest basic variation, the kiteloop *to blind*. A rider with enough power in his kite who pulls himself towards the *bar* fast and a little more aggressively can quickly turn this manoeuvre into a kiteloop handlepass.

As in the normal *unhooked* kiteloop, Kristin flies the kite at 12 o'clock, unhooks and quickly reaches backwards with both hands. As soon as the kite starts the looping motion she goes to windward and takes off. Following the pull of the kite, she goes into a *railey*, but

must then prepare to land *blind* as soon as the kite starts flying towards the zenith again. To do this, she releases her back hand from the *bar*, looks backwards and lands backwards. Kristin has to absorb the landing well with her knees and ensure that she is riding behind the kite, and she lands on an extreme downwind course. To prevent the kite from going immediately into the next loop, Kristin passes the *bar* around her back as quickly as possible.

Key points for mental imaging:
- Kite at 12 o'clock and unhook
- Reach back with both hands and take off with the first pull of the kite
- Remain in railey position until kite flies back upwards
- Take back hand off bar, turn with back in landing direction and look backwards
- Land and cushion softly with knees
- Quickly pass bar round and control kite.

Passing the *bar* behind the back can form the final element of an unhooked jump back on the surface of the water or it can be the object of the manoeuvre itself, as is the case with the air pass, for example. Surface passes can generally be performed even without a preceding jump. With a preceding trick the surface pass is naturally more complex and thus more attractive. It's also helpful that a jump executed first and ending on a broad reach takes the tension out of the lines, due to which the surface pass is without pressure and can thus be performed more easily. All handlepass manoeuvres put considerable strain on the shoulders, and so longer-term preparation, as illustrated in Chapter 9, "Training ashore – building up strength", is recommended here.

Handlepasses

- **Railey to revert surface pass**
- **Railey to blind surface pass**
- **Back to blind surface pass**
- **Front to blind surface pass**
- **Railey to wrapped surface pass**
- **Back to wrapped surface pass**
- **Front to wrapped surface pass**
- **Blind judge**
- **Air pass**

Tip: Surface passes out of a *toeside* landing are the easiest and are recommended for getting into this trick category. They can be combined with *unhooked* tricks like a small jump, a *railey* or a front- or backflip, or they can just be performed while riding by bearing away strongly. Kristin demonstrates the basic *railey* variation:

Railey to revert surface pass

Kristin approaches the jump *unhooked* with her kite in the 1 o'clock position, holding the *bar* in the middle. To generate a strong line tension and thus energy for the take-off, she goes hard to windward. She takes off powerfully and goes into a body stretch, allowing herself to be pulled behind her kite in the air. She brings the board above head height by raising her legs. To prepare for landing, Kristin pulls on the *bar* again and pulls the board underneath her body, turning the board to the *toeside* position, i.e. the left leg,

which was the back leg on take off, is leading after landing. She lands *toeside*. In doing this she takes her right hand off the *bar*, which enables her to turn her upper body towards the tail. She carries on turning until she can reach the *bar* again behind her back with her right hand. Then she quickly lets go with the left hand and at the same time begins to turn her board further around. As she finishes turning, she places her left hand back on the *bar* and continues riding heelside.

Key points for mental imaging:
- Take off unhooked with kite at 1 or 11 o'clock
- Pull legs up behind
- Land on toeside and let go with back hand
- Reach with rear hand around back and turn body
- Pass bar round back
- Continue turning board and follow up.

125

Surface passes landed *to blind* are harder, since the landing *to blind* has to be mastered reliably for this. To learn these moves, first the preceding trick can be landed on the backside edge and then a surface pass via *blind* added on. This way the movement imagery for the landing can be improved and the movement sequence learnt faster through mental imaging and then applied on the water. It is particularly important with landings *to*

blind that the rider looks behind in advance, in order to bring the body into the correct position, and that pressure is transferred to the new back leg in good time, to absorb the landing. In the following three sequences Kristin demonstrates the basic tricks *to blind*.

Until just before landing, Kristin does a normal *railey* (see above). Then, however, she takes her right and rear hand off the *bar*, which she holds in the centre with her left hand, and turns her board while still in flight into the *blind* position. It's important to look back here. Upon

Railey to blind

contact with the surface of the water *to blind*, she bends her upper body well forwards, to cushion the landing and to be able to put pressure on the leg. In this position she continues to turn her right shoulder until she can reach the *bar* behind her back. Then she releases it with the left hand and turns until she can reach the *bar* again with her left hand too. The moment at which Kristin takes hold of the *bar* with both hands again, she turns the board back into the normal riding position.

Key points for mental imaging:
• Take off unhooked with kite at 45°
• Pull legs up behind
• Let go backhand, look backwards
• Land board to blind
• Bend upper body forwards, cushion landing
• Pass bar to right behind back
• Let go left and turn
• Follow up left and turn board.

surface pass

Back to blind

As in all other handlepass jumps, Kristin approaches this trick *unhooked* on a reach, flying her kite with her hands centred on the *bar* between the 10 and 11 o'clock position. She goes hard to windward to take off over the back, right leg. She starts to rotate as soon as she takes off with the aid of momentum from the middle of her body and by twisting her head. After a rotation, she stops the movement and rotates back by moving her head in the opposite direction and taking her right hand off the *bar*. She lands *to blind* on a broad reach. Upon landing, Kristin bends her upper body well forward, to be able to cushion the landing well. Then she reaches for the *bar* behind her back with her right hand. Once she has taken hold of it securely, she immediately releases the left hand. She can then continue rotating and grasp the *bar* with both hands.

128

Key points for mental imaging:
- Unhook, hands on middle of the bar
- Take off and execute a rotation backwards
- Stop rotation with the aid of the head movement and rotate 180° back, release right hand
- Land to blind and upper body forwards
- Pass bar behind back
- Carry on turning upper body and place left hand back on bar.

Tip: In the first stage, the landing *to blind* from rotations can be practised first hooked-in and with kite steering. Only later does it make sense to practise these landings from powered jumps. This trick is best practised in light, constant wind.

surface pass

For this jump too Kristin flies her kite *unhooked* between 10 and 11 o'clock for take-off. She edges to windward for take-off and goes straight into a forward rotation. Here she pulls her legs up slightly to speed up the rotation somewhat. After the 360° front rotation Kristin takes her rear hand off the *bar*, but rotates another 180° to land the jump *to blind*. It is important that after the 360° front rotation she briefly focuses on the landing point, but then looks backwards to get into the right body position for a powerful *blind* landing. She cushions the landing with her knees and her upper body bent forward and then immediately has to grip the *bar* with her right hand behind her back. Then she lets go with the left hand, carries on turning, and grips the *bar* with both hands.

The third and last surface pass option is that executed with a *wrapped* landing. Even if a *wrapped* landing looks at first sight like a landing *to blind*, it isn't by any means. If you intend to land *wrapped*, it will probably be easier to do so on the opposite tack to which you normally land *blind*, with the other hand on the bar. The *wrapped* landing is actually an over-rotated landing *to toeside*. Here Kristin shows the three basic *wrapped moves*.

Key points for mental imaging:
- Take off unhooked with hands centered on the bar
- Immediately start rotation
- Release right hand before landing
- Land to blind and cushion
- Pass bar behind the back
- Continue turning upper body and left hand back on bar
- Ride away.

Front to blind

surface pass

Railey to wrapped surface pass

For this trick, Kristin takes off as in the normal *railey* with the kite at 45° and lets herself be pulled behind her kite. When the tension on the lines eases a little at the highest point of the jump, she pulls herself towards the *bar* and begins to turn. First she rotates the board as if she wanted to land *toeside*, and then rotates a half turn further, taking her front hand off the *bar* and putting her centre of gravity over the board. She uses the free hand to help her through the rotation.

She absorbs the landing with her knees. Upon landing her back arm is now half wrapped around her body. To be able to cushion the landing and pass the *bar* around to the leading hand, she bends her body forward slightly. Finally she

passes the *bar* behind her back to her right hand, continues to rotate and puts both hands on the bar.

Key points for mental imaging:
- Unhook and take off with hands in the middle of the bar
- Stretch body out
- Pull actively towards bar and let go with front hand
- Rotate 180° degrees past toeside
- Land to wrapped and upper body forward
- Pass bar behind back
- Carry on turning upper body and other hand back on bar.

Back to wrapped surface pass

Kristin approaches this trick *unhooked* on a reach and flies her kite between the 1 and 2 o'clock position with her hands in the middle of the *bar*. She goes hard to windward and takes off using the back, left leg. As she takes off she initiates the backward rotation with the aid of her core strength and the movement of her head. After one full rotation she takes her front, right hand off the *bar*, briefly spots her landing point for orientation purposes and thus gets an idea of how far the last part of the turn has to be taken. Now she rotates 180° further. For the *wrapped* landing on a slight broad reach she bends her upper body well forward. After landing she reaches behind her back for the *bar* with her right hand. Once she has a firm hold on it, she immediately lets go with the left hand. She can then carry on rotating and grasp the *bar* with both hands.

Key points for mental imaging:
- Kite at 45° and unhook
- Start backward rotation
- After full rotation release front hand from the bar and rotate 180° further
- Prepare for wrapped landing, look back and release bar
- Land wrapped
- On the water pass the bar behind the back
- Rotate to end and ride away.

Tip: Before progressing to practising this trick on the water, it is advised that you visualize a *back to toeside* with an additional half turn, which ends in a backward landing with the arms '*wrapped around you*'.

Front to wrapped surface pass

Kristin approaches this trick *unhooked* on a reach. She flies the kite in the 45° position with her hands in the middle of the *bar*. She cuts upwind and takes off over the back, left leg. Immediately upon take-off she starts the forward rotation, aided by head movement. After a ¾-rotation she takes her leading hand off the *bar*, stops rotating with the help of her head movement, due to which rotation back

by half a turn is initiated, and then lands *wrapped,* i.e. with the back hand on the *bar* around her body. Upon landing she bends her upper body well forward and she reaches behind her back with her leading, right hand on the *bar*. Once she has a firm hold on it, she releases the left hand immediately and can then ride away normally.

Key points for mental imaging:
- Kite at 45° and unhook
- Start forward rotation
- Stop rotating after ¾-rotation, release leading hand and rotate ½-rotation back
- Prepare wrapped landing, look backwards
- Land wrapped
- Pass bar behind back on the water
- Ride away.

Blind judge

Kristin flies her kite at 45°, unhooks and goes briefly upwind to build up considerable momentum for a strong take-off. She follows the kite in a *railey*. At the highest point of the jump she then initiates a flat 360°. As she does this she very quickly pulls herself to the *bar* and lets go of it with her back hand to assist her in the rotation. Now she reaches with her rear hand behind her back for the *bar*, so as to make the pass while still in the air. As soon as she is able to grip the *bar* with her rear hand, she releases the other (leading) hand and lands *toeside*. Now she has time to return both hands to the *bar* and to *switch* the board back into the normal (heelside) riding position.

Key points for mental imaging:
- **Kite at 45°, unhook and take off**
- **Go into a railey**
- **At the highest point quickly pull towards bar**
- **Release back arm, rotate 360° flat spin**
- **Pass bar behind back**
- **Land toeside and ride away.**

Air pass

Although the air pass doesn't really look like it, it's the easiest and most attainable aerial handlepass to begin with. It is performed with kite steering and can be combined with forward and backward rotations. Once these tricks can be landed, it's possible to fly the kite lower when performing them, thereby adding greater power to the jumps.

As well as mental imaging, which the rider can use to rehearse the action sequence in his head, practising tricks of this kind on dry land is advised in order to visualize the manoeuvre and attune the muscles to this load.

Phases 6–9 of the air pass show the heavily twisted position of the shoulders, which once again underlines the necessity of strengthening the shoulder muscles (for strengthening of the rotator cuff see Chapter 9 "Training ashore – building up strength").

But now to the trick:

The jump should be high enough so that you will have sufficient airtime to perform the trick. To achieve this, Kristin performs this trick with kite support. She flies the kite in the 11 o'clock position and unhooks. She holds the *bar* in the middle, edges hard to windward and steers the kite into the 12 o'clock position. In phases 2 to 4, one might think that Kristin was preparing to perform a 360° turn on the parallel bar (a comparison that can assist with visualization): aided by the pop and board momentum, she pulls herself up close to the *bar*, bending her legs as she does so. Here she brings her rear hip as close as possible to the *bar*, simultaneously bringing the board above head height and her head downwards, In this position Kristin releases her leading, left hand from the *bar* and rotates quickly around her own axis, gripping the *bar* with her other

hand, behind her back. She then hangs from her outstretched arm with her left hand below the *bar* and turns her body back in the riding direction. To achieve greater body tension and make the landing easier, she returns her left hand also to the *bar* and can now stop the rotation and spot the landing. She absorbs the landing with her knees. If it were a slightly greater distance to the beach, Kristin would pull her kite further forward for the landing.

Key points for mental imaging:
- Take off energetically unhooked and with kite steering
- Using the momentum from board and body, bring hips up to bar
- Board above head height, release leading hand and rotate quickly
- Pass bar behind back
- Release rear hand
- Hang from left hand and bring body into landing position
- Bring other hand back to bar and land.

140

Air pass practice on dry land.

You don't have to be 'riding giants' to enjoy the sense of elation that riding waves with a small kiteboard gives you. On the contrary: being able to ride small waves dynamically at high speed is difficult from the timing point of view and gives you this special surf sensation that occurs when your actions match the wave exactly. The feeling of experiencing nature and its power so directly in this way is something wonderful that connects all surfers, whether they use a kite or not.

All wave-riding begins with finding a good wave, positioning yourself on that wave and using its speed to ride towards the shore. Then the first bottom turn is made, the kiter rides into the wave trough, lies into the turn and rides back to its breaking edge, the curl, where it has the most energy, to make a carve in the upper part of the wave with a top turn or a cut back.

Note: Wave-kiting is a whole chapter in itself. We will only be able to touch briefly on the topic in the following few pages. You will find the most basic wave moves that will get you started in the waves and you might want to explore a little more of wave-riding than we can show you here.

- **Bottom turn**
- **Top turn/Cut back**
- **Aerial**

Riding waves

Bottom turn

Seen from the shore, the wind blows *sideshore* from the left in this bottom turn, so that Marc rides the wave to leeward with his right foot forward (*goofy*). He flies the kite with his leading, right hand in the middle of the *bar*. Before making the turn to leeward and back towards the wave, he steers the kite in this direction to keep sufficient tension in the lines. He initiates the bottom turn by turning his upper body and shifting his weight towards the centre of the turn, thereby leaning so far inwards that he can drag the hand on the inside of the turn through the water. He observes the development of the wave, as the radius of the turn is geared to this; the timing is crucial for the success of the ensuing cutback or top turn. Before Marc rides back to the wave, he steers his kite back in the opposite direction so as to get enough pressure in the kite to support the following top turn, the start of which can be seen in the last picture.

Note: Marc is riding *unhooked* here. This is the more advanced way of doing these moves. You will want to try the moves while hooked-in for a while first and then later try them *unhooked* for a different style.

Key points for mental imaging:
- Kite back towards 10 or 2 o'clock
- Lie into the turn towards the wave
- Hand on inside of turn towards curve middle
- At end of bottom turn steer kite back ...

Top turn/Cut back

Marc performs this cut back in the steepest part of the wave at the point where it's just beginning to break. Thus the maximum energy is available to him, which he utilizes for a very dynamic turn back into the wave trough. Before reaching the lip of the wave he has already steered his kite back into the new riding direction to the 1 to 2 o'clock position. At the apex of the curve he shifts his centre of gravity back and turns his board using his rear, left leg.

Key points for mental imaging
for a bottom turn with subsequent top turn:
- Kite back towards 10 or 2 o'clock
- Lie into curve
- Hand on inside of turn towards curve middle
- At end of bottom turn steer kite back to 2 or 10 o'clock
- Just before wave lip change edge and edge hard on back edge on inside of turn
- Weight forwards again
- Turn kite and approach next bottom turn ...

 Aerial

This trick differs from the cut back in that the kiter rides out of the bottom turn at high speed so precisely into the just-breaking wave that the lip of the wave can be used as a small take-off ramp. In this *aerial* Marc has already steered the kite clearly in the new riding direction above the 2 o'clock position before reaching the wave lip, thereby increasing the energy for take-off from the highest part of the wave. He flies a short distance towards the wave trough and lands on the breaking wave in order to then ride away on it to leeward.

Key points for mental imaging:
- Kite back towards 10 or 2 o'clock
- Lie into carve
- Hand on inside of turn to curve middle
- At end of bottom turn steer kite back to 2 or 10 o'clock
- Steer board straight just before wave lip and pop from wave lip
- Weight forwards
- Land.

Tip 1: To learn wave-riding it makes sense to look for small, slow waves at first, to practise coordinating board and kite steering. In bigger waves the turns can be practised initially in the 'green' part of the wave, where it is not yet so steep.

Tip 2: In *side-offshore wind* virtually no kite steering is needed for wave-riding, and so you can give the wave your full attention. With a *side-on-* to *side-shore wind,* kite steering can be practised in the wave.

AFTER KITING IS

The title of this section is based loosely on the training philosophy of Sepp Herberger, manager of the West German national football team which won the World Cup in 1954: 'After the game is before the game'.

In this section we offer recommendations as to what you should do directly after kiting and what measures you should take in the time between training sessions on the water, a period that can extend over weeks and months.

7 'Cool down': cooling down after training on the water

It must be pointed out once again here that kitesurfing subjects your body to high physical stresses. The longer the training session on the water and the higher the level of fatigue resulting from this and from one's level of fitness, the greater is the necessity for a cooling-down phase. This is because during kiting and the varied and sometimes very strenuous muscle activity associated with it, metabolic by-products accumulate in the muscles and these have to be removed by the blood. Nutrients that facilitate fresh muscular activity have to be supplied, which is likewise accomplished via the circulation. It's obvious, therefore, that the circulation has to be maintained to accelerate this process. Following an exhausting and exhilarating session on the water, however, most kiters unfortunately give in to the urge to flop instantly into a camping chair or lie in a hammock, with the following consequences: the metabolic by-products remain in the muscles and make the arms and legs feel really 'heavy'.

The recommended cooling-down programme is as follows: active regeneration can commence with an easy run to cool down and to keep the blood flowing at a slightly higher rate. This helps to slow the bodily functions down gradually rather than abruptly. The duration of this activity recommended by sports medicine experts is between **5 and 20 minutes**. The sooner the cooling-down run follows the exertion, the more effective it is, i.e. it should be carried out immediately after changing. Light **stretching** of the muscle elements subjected to particular stress lowers the tonicity and facilitates metabolic processes. After this, further regeneration activities such as a **sauna** or **massage** speed up the recovery process even more. In addition, to prevent protein synthesis, which would set in if no energy is supplied and would attack muscle mass to gain energy, **carbohydrates** should be taken on board as soon as possible following the training session. It probably goes without saying that as much **liquid** as possible should be taken in, but not in the form of beer or other alcohol.

If you follow these recommendations, you'll discover how good it is to be fit enough again the following day to set a new training goal. Going out on the water again with well-regenerated muscles enhances your performance and thus enjoyment, and minimizes the risk of injury. It's not for nothing that nearly all professional sportsmen and many amateurs from other sporting disciplines, have long since integrated this approach following the actual sport into their training plan. Anyone not sufficiently satisfied by the physiological reasons can simply experience the beneficial feeling produced by cooling down on the beach after a good day's kitesurfing; that can be motivation enough.

BEFORE KITING

8 The crossover effect: using related sports disciplines

Aaron Hadlow, one of the world champions, goes wakeboarding. Ex-world champion Cindy Mosey rides a mountain bike and snowboards, as does Kristin. Mike Blomval is a good in-line skater. Madison van Heurk and Andre Phillip surf, and one of the best kitesurfers in the world at present, Alvaro Onieva, is a skateboarder. If asked why they do it, most of them would answer that they enjoy it. Be that as it may, what is particularly interesting about this when it comes to designing a kitesurfing training programme is that it's not surprising to find that these are all sports with a similar profile of requirements to kitesurfing. Other sports accordingly exhibit similarity with regard to the muscle groups used, which are controlled by the motor centre in the central nervous system, and with regard to the sensory units that continually provide the athlete with information on the position of his body in relation to his surroundings. The proven and known effect of learning transfer consists in the fact that mastering one of these disciplines makes it easier to learn a similar sport (proactive transfer). For example, someone who can snowboard or windsurf will find it relatively easy to learn how to kitesurf, because he can transfer the experience acquired to the new sport to be learned.

This effect is described as a 'crossover'

or 'transfer'. For experienced kitesurfers, the following discovery is no less interesting: if a new sport is learned, the experience gained from this can also have a positive effect on sports mastered previously (retroactive transfer). An athlete learning to snowboard after having learned how to kitesurf will practise his balancing ability under different conditions and can, e.g. improve his feel

Complementary sport in one's kite-free time.

Yoga improves bodily perception and awareness, strength and mobility.

for the board in kitesurfing thanks to the different edging options that arise in snowboarding. The frontside turn in snowboarding calls for a shift in weight and edging very similar to the tack *into switch*, just as the backside turn is virtually identical to the tack *from switch* in this respect. To make this transfer of learning useful, however, the athlete must be capable of differentiating between the common features and the differences. Otherwise it would make sense to practise precisely this bodily perception to start with. Kristin has chosen yoga as a type of sport that teaches bodily sensation to a special level, but other sports such as judo and other Budo disciplines (associated with body recognition) are suitable in this context.

Which sports, then, are the close or more distant relations of kitesurfing that are capable of being transferred and can therefore provide satisfactory support for the training programme outside the kiting season? To be able to answer this question, it's a good idea first to identify the abilities that are considered essential for kitesurfing. By this we mean the perceptual abilities as well as the coordinative abilities.

The perception of balance or equilibrium and the imminent loss of this is a perceptual ability in which items of information from various 'perceptual channels' (in this case kinaesthetic and vestibular) are collated and 'offset' against one another at lightning speed, the result being an indication of whether, and in what form, compensatory movements are required to remain in equilibrium. These compensatory movements are then the motor consequence of the perceived imminent loss of balance. The coordinative ability of balance accordingly comprises the perception of a lack of equilibrium and the rapid motor reaction to it. If, in addition to simply riding and various tricks, you visualize a landing *to blind*, then it becomes clear how high the demands made on the **ability to balance** are in kitesurfing. Thus balancing ability is probably the most obvious prerequisite for kitesurfing, although there is a fundamental difference to be observed here from the ability to balance in other sport disciplines. Due to the positioning of the foot straps on the board, the kitesurfer assumes a fixed foot position, causing him to make different compensatory movements from inline skaters or skiers, for example, who can put their legs in a different position in relation to one another to maintain their balance. Kitesurfers are no more able to do this than snowboarders, wakeboarders or windsurfers; surfers and skateboarders are rather more flexible in this respect, as although their feet are mostly in a fixed position on the board, they are not strapped down. In all these board disci-

plines, movements to maintain balance are executed by the torso in conjunction with the upper limbs. As season- and weather-dependent as all these sports may be, the opportunity often arises nevertheless to use one of these types of sports for cross-training. If this isn't possible, there are supplementary pieces of training equipment such as the wobble board, for example, which have proved of value for all these sports. Although not very similar to kitesurfing, balance training on, e.g. a unicycle is particularly challenging. Admittedly, riding a unicycle is not especially similar to skiing either, but they have been used successfully by professional skiers for complementary training purposes.

As soon as they embark on the first rotation jumps, every kitesurfer realizes how great the importance of **orientation ability** is for this sport. When it comes to the difficulty involved in orienting oneself in different planes during the rotations, kitesurfing surpasses the sports of snowboarding, freestyle skiing and windsurfing: both in rotation jumps via kicker and in the half pipe with the snowboard or skis and in all windsurfing loops, gravity acts in relation to the momentum of the take-off, which is, however, a readily calculable variable. In kitesurfing, the pull of the kite on the body of the athlete acts in addition to these two variables throughout the rotation and pulls him in a direction opposing the gravitational force. In addition, if the kitesurfer 'mis-steers' the kite a little during the turn, it becomes increasingly difficult to set these influencing parameters off against one another, which could result in him becoming disoriented in the truest sense of the word. (For this reason the rotation jumps are introduced in Chapter 6 by the backflip, without kite steering.) Since this does not occur in such a manner in other sports, it is correspondingly difficult to advise on sensible cross-training. We followed the half pipe snowboarders and got several ideas for developing or improving orientation ability through

trampoline jumping with rotations. Anyone wishing to add water as an element can also perform somersaults from the one- or three-metre board in the swimming pool. However, in relation to kitesurfing these are only of limited assistance in developing orientation ability, for the reasons set out above. Wakeboarding offers the most complex training, but with regard to orientation only if rotation jumps are used. However, since wakeboards and kiteboards are of virtually identical construction, riding in itself can be practised on the wakeboard on days when there is no wind, as can kitesurfing tricks in the wakeboard style.

Wakeboarding can therefore undoubtedly be counted as one of the close relations of kitesurfing, additionally because various partial body movements have to be brought together in a complete body movement in wakeboarding, just as in kitesurfing. For example, the pressure on a board edge is introduced by turning the head and the torso and the momentum is transmitted via the legs to the board. This interaction, which is perfectly coordinated in time, is termed **combinatory ability** and becomes even clearer when considering the take-off: edging of the board must be precisely coordinated in time with steering the kite back and pulling on the *bar*. Naturally all these types of momentum must be realized in a suitably regulated manner, which is why **differential ability** is cited as an essential requirement for sensitive and powerful kitesurfing. All types of sports in which changes of direction are accomplished on a piece of sports equipment by combining momentum are suitable for cross-training; sports in which the position on the board is identical to that in kitesurfing are especially suitable here, as described above.

The **reactive ability** and the **adaptive ability** occur in all common sense sports, which include extreme sports and thus also kitesurfing. The athlete engaging in a common sense sport must recognize a change in the environmental conditions,

148

make a decision regarding an action and then carry this out. In kitesurfing, this sequence can be triggered by a squall blowing in, a continuously changing wave, or simply by another water-sports athlete suddenly popping up. As well as in the sports addressed above, these basic elements occur in most ball sports, which can be included among the more distant relations. On the beach, beach volleyball and soccer seem obvious choices as a means of cross-training.

Conclusion: Wind isn't always necessary to practise for kitesurfing. All the essential prerequisites or skills can be practised using other more or less related sports disciplines. The most similar, and thus highly recommended complementary sport, is wakeboarding, while skateboarding has proved its worth as the easiest cross-training that can be integrated into everyday life.

Wakeboarding – very similar to kiting.

⑨ *Training ashore* 149

In all sports, athletes, in addition to engaging in the sport itself, undertake training that supports the sport. The aim of this is to improve their basic physical abilities and thereby to create a basis for optimizing their performance in the respective sport.

BUILDING UP STRENGTH

Every sport has its own profile of requirements, both with regard to the necessary coordinative abilities, as described in the last chapter, and in respect of the muscle groups that are most heavily involved. This means that strength training specific to the particular sport is required.

Building up kitesurf-specific strength: why?

Practised at regular intervals and for the right amount of time, kitesurfing itself is very good training for core stability. But kiting is an extreme sport in which athletes are heavily dependent on the weather conditions, meaning that regular training sessions of the right duration are difficult to organize. This means that kiters should be physically well-prepared to seize kitesurfing opportunities when they arise. For one thing, kitesurfing is more fun if the kiter is physically fit, as more tricks are successful when the rider can maintain coordination. For another thing, the risk of serious injury is minimized, as is the risk of sustaining physical damage. Various aspects should

be taken into account in this regard.

Kitesurfers ride on a pretty small, wobbly board in a moving element. As a result, the forces acting on the kitesurfer are changing constantly, causing him to make small or large compensatory movements continuously. In most cases these compensatory movements are not even conscious movements, although they sometimes call for a high strength input. They're controlled by processes in the central nervous system (consisting of the brain and the spinal cord): muscles, tendons and joints report the condition of our body with reference to the forces acting on it to the central nervous system via sensors. The central nervous system processes these signals at lightning speed and triggers the appropriate movements. Thus not only is a good perceptual capacity of the participating muscles, joints and tendons called for, but the muscles involved must also possess the strength potential to be able to perform these rapid compensatory movements. This interaction of perception and movement can and should be practised not only out on the water during the actual kiting session, but also by means of suitable exercises when preparing for the season and during the season itself. Kitesurfers should always endeavour to extend their strength potential in conjunction with improving their balance and joint functions, because in kiting it isn't big muscles that we need, but intelligent muscles. Training that addresses these automatic compensatory movements not only develops kite performance but is also a particularly suitable injury prophylaxis, because a well-trained neuromuscular (interaction between the muscles and the nerve tracts supplying them) system is better able to protect

itself. The resistance level of areas like tendons, which are poorly supplied with blood and are put under high stress in kiting, can also be increased by this type of training.

Kitesurfing is a sport that puts a heavy strain on the musculoskeletal system. The kitesurfer's body must withstand the entire gamut of forces originating from the transfer of energy from the kite to the board.

This is accomplished in particular by the upper and lower back muscles. The results of this transfer are propulsion and forces that become effective for a high-energy and economical take-off. Not only the big muscle groups that we are accustomed to exercising in the gym but also and in particular the small muscles that support the hips, torso, shoulders and back are extremely important in this process. As described above, these should be strengthened in conjunction with balancing skills, for the supporting core muscles form the pillars of our strength

and are the basis for all movements.

Targeted improvement of our strength capacity plays a large part in helping to avoid acute injuries and secondary damage as well as in improving our kiting performance. Being able to take off powerfully and economically requires a suitably developed level of strength as well as good technique.

Building up kitesurf-specific strength: how?

To be able to kitesurf with greater stability and more strength, a training regimen is recommended that calls for scarcely any equipment apart from a Thera-Band. Up to an hour of training should be undertaken three times a week. The objective is to lay the foundations for powerful and functional movements, and to maintain or extend these foundations. Due to the fact that it is **not** body parts but body movements that are being trained, a level of functional strength corresponding to the sport's profile of requirements is developed.

During the kiting season, strengthening of the basic muscles involved in kiting results from practising the sport itself. The best condition training for kiting is kiting! But it should be remembered here that the training sessions should not be too long, as is often seen to be the case (see Chapter 2 "Structuring a training unit"). On the days and in the weeks between training sessions on the water during the season, the muscles that bear the brunt of the work in kitesurfing should be strengthened further to prevent damaging joint stresses. This objective should be pursued specifically in the athlete's kite-free time. Continual exercising of all the core muscles will reduce the susceptibility of the spinal column to injury, and long-term back problems will be avoided. Stronger core muscles can also enhance performance, including that of the limbs, since limb movements also start from the torso. A trick like the *board-off*, for example, is impossible without suitably developed core muscles.

The exercises listed all have a strong proprioceptive (proprioception (from 'proprio' = own and 'perception')) requirement and so they improve proprioception in addition to strength potential, with a resulting positive effect on kiting performance. The instability of a small kiteboard leads to the body making an effort via the internal feedback system described to produce stability through constant, rapid compensatory movements. To do this, it utilizes the many small muscles and especially the interaction between these.

For kitesurfing it's necessary both to support muscle development that is equal to the load imposed – in particular to protect joints from injury and unilateral pressures – and to practise muscular endurance (this strength component is influenced in turn by the level of maximum strength, to which attention must therefore be devoted), so as to be able to withstand the stress on the water for as long as possible. The following guide values apply when assigning these types of training:

– Muscle development training by means of 12 to15 repeats at approximately 60% of maximum power

– Muscular endurance training by means of 15 to 30 repeats at approximately 40% of maximum power.

In the following section, exercises are shown that are intended to make the training programme clear. Further exercises can be found in the programmes listed in the bibliography.

Core stability

As already mentioned, kitesurfing subjects the torso to heavy loads. To develop the power of the limbs, a physiologically satisfactory posture of the torso with well-developed muscles is also required to be able to maintain the static positions when kiting straight ahead and to hold suitable body positions dynamically in jumps and other tricks.

Back muscles (cf. Verstegen, 2006: p. 74 'Spinal stability')

Strengthening the back muscles and improving balance at the same time:

'Rear leg lift': In this exercise the body should be held in a straight line from head to foot. The exercise can be intensified by using two stones of equal weight as a substitute for dumb-bells.

Strengthening the back muscles:

From a position lying on your back, lift the pelvis and then extend the lower leg away parallel to the knee. It i's important to flex the foot towards your nose. Hold the resulting position shown here for two seconds, then lower and repeat the exercise with the other leg.

151

Strengthening the core, hips and shoulders:

In this exercise, too, the body should form a straight line from head to foot. Raise one arm and the opposite leg, hold for two seconds and then swap arm and leg over. This exercise can be performed twice over 30 to 40 seconds.

Strengthening the back, abdominal and glute muscles:
The three variations shown differ in level of difficulty. As your level of fitness improves, a more advanced level can be selected.

152

Variation 1:   Variation 2:   Variation 3:

Hold the position shown for 20 seconds, or perform 10 repeats of 2 seconds each.

Abdominal muscles

When exercising the abdominal muscles, the feet should not be held down or wedged, as otherwise it would be the hip flexors that were being exercised instead.

Strengthening the upper abdominal muscles:

Lift the shoulder blades slightly, stretching the arms forwards or holding them to the sides of the head by the ears (but not by the back of the neck).

Strengthening the lower abdominal muscles:

Lift the legs at right angles and press the arms down onto the mat. Raise the pelvis by pushing your knees upwards, but don't draw the knees down towards your chest! This position can be held for 15 to 20 seconds.

Arm and shoulder muscles

Most of the exercises for strengthening the shoulders and arms are done standing on one leg, in order to practise balance, which is important in kiting, as well as the associated strength component. Thus these exercises unite conditioning and coordinative abilities (cf. Nagel & Spreckels, 2003: p. 213). The proprioception of the muscles, joints and tendons can be improved in this way, which not only reduces the risk of injury when kitesurfing but also improves sensitive movement.

The exercises are started with a lightly tensioned Thera-Band, which should not be slack during the exercise, as the tension ensures the joint-tightening effect. The resistance is chosen so that the fatigue can be felt clearly in the relevant muscles after carrying out the exercise.

The **shoulder** and **chest muscles** are exposed to particularly high levels of strain, which becomes noticeable when riding and especially when performing handlepasses. Often a disparity exists between the rotators and the deltoid muscle, which can be partly responsible for impingement syndrome (noticeable due to pain when raising the arm laterally), a functional impairment of the shoulder joint. Regular strengthening of the rotators should therefore also be undertaken.

Strengthening the rotators:
In this exercise to strengthen the rotator cuff, clamp an object, e.g. a bottle of sunscreen, between the elbow and the torso. This prevents the deltoid muscle from assuming a large portion of the work and guarantees that only the rotators are exercised. The movement is from inside to outside against the resistance of the Thera-Band.

154

Strengthening the upper back and shoulder muscles:
In this exercise, Kristin fastens the Thera-Band to a tree and pulls either with both arms (the bar can also be tied on for this purpose) at the same time or alternately with one arm and then the other against the resistance. The elbows should be drawn back at shoulder height; avoid rotating the upper body when doing this.

Bicep exercise:
The upper arm flexors are also heavily stressed in kitesurfing, so here too strengthening with a neuromuscular component is recommended. Kristin stands on one leg with the Thera-Band under the same foot. She bends both arms alternately with suitable tension on the Thera-Band.

Pull-ups
Pull-ups are also very suitable. To simulate kitesurfing in the strengthening exercise, the grip should correspond to the kiter's hold on the bar. In order to prepare for the strain imposed by many jumps, pull-ups with both hands directly adjacent to one another should also be performed.

Strengthening the antagonist muscles:

The term 'antagonist muscles' is used here to describe those muscles that are under less stress in kiting. To clarify which muscles are actually involved, two forms of training for antagonist muscle elements are shown. It makes sense to exercise these muscle elements in order to stress the shoulders uniformly and thereby increase their resistance. In addition, when exercising the antagonist muscle, the agonist – which is the muscle that is strongly stressed in kiting – is extended, an action that counters shortening, and thus possible problems. A good time to exercise the antagonist muscles to achieve the best results is on days when you have been kiting.

The forearm and shoulder muscles:

In this exercise Kristin stands on one leg on the Thera-Band and brings her arms upwards in front of her body under the tension of the Thera-Band.

Strengthening the lateral shoulder muscles:

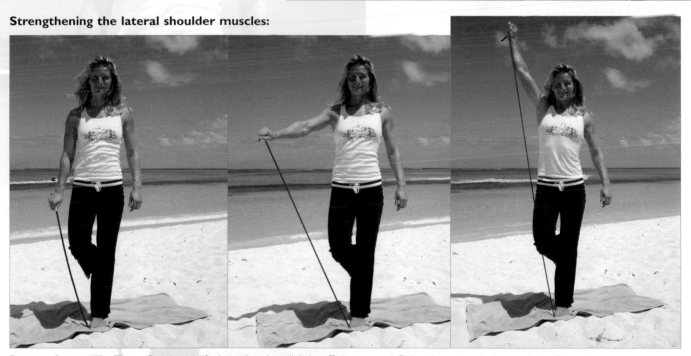

Put one foot on the Thera-Band and lift the other leg slightly off the ground. Raise the extended arms laterally upwards in front of the upper body. At the end of the movement, the thumbs should be pointing upwards.

Press-ups:

Do press-ups on an exercise ball or other unstable base.

Leg muscles

By strengthening the leg muscles you achieve stability of the joints, especially of the knee joint, which is subject to heavy pressure on landings. Doing the exercises standing on one leg means that the strengthening is accompanied by an improvement in balancing ability and proprioception.

Strengthening the hip muscles and the supporting leg:

The free leg is moved outwards against the resistance of the Thera-Band; only the free leg should move, the upper body should remain steady.

156

Strengthening the hips and leg muscles in conjunction with balance:

In this exercise it's important not to touch the ground with the back knee and to straighten up the body powerfully and quickly from the hip and legs. As a result, Kristin finds herself with her front leg briefly in the air, then absorbing the energy low down in the squat with the other leg and building it up again. To intensify the effect of this exercise, hold two stones of equal weight in your hands as substitute dumb-bells.

Neuromuscular training

In many sports, the number of injuries seen, especially of the knee joint, has fallen substantially thanks to the use of neuromuscular training. A study of handball players has demonstrated this impressively (cf. Petersen et al., 2002: pp. 122–126). Because, as we have already said, balancing ability is very important in kiting and the study in question highlights the importance of proprioceptive training for the prevention of injuries, especially of the lower limbs (28% foot, 13% knee of all injuries in kitesurfing; see Chapter 1 "Safety first"), such training should be included without fail in your training programme. The strengthening exercises described above already have a high proprioceptive and neuromuscular content, but a wide variety of additional options exists for training in this sphere. In all exercises in which the aim is to practise balancing skills, the proprioceptive element can be increased by closing the eyes when doing the exercises. Here are a few exercises to try:

Balancing on the 'wobble board':

- on both legs
- on one leg
- on both legs with eyes closed
- on one leg with eyes closed
- on one or both legs with an additional task, such as catching and throwing, or firing back a ball thrown at you.

Jumps from a small elevation onto a soft floor mat or the sand:

- on both legs
- on one leg
- on both legs with eyes closed
- on one leg with eyes closed.

Training of this kind, if carried out on an ongoing basis and at suitable intervals between training on the water, is highly effective in preventing ankle joint and knee injuries. This is due to the fact that the body learns to react to external influences by means of quick compensatory movements. Take the landing to blind, for example, which didn't acquire its name without a reason: this landing is extremely difficult, as the landing point cannot be seen but has to be sensed. On initial contact with the water, the neuromuscular system immediately instigates small compensatory movements that make it possible for the rider to maintain his balance. Thus it's not surprising that improving neuromuscular interaction enables the landing to blind, among other manoeuvres, to be managed more often and more reliably.

Endurance training

It has been shown that people with a good endurance capacity suffer from fewer back problems. This fact alone is recommendation enough for endurance training. As described in Chapter 1, "Safety first", kitesurfers are often troubled by injuries to the ankle joint and knee joint, mostly caused by landings. Flat landings and landings with the knees straight increase the pressure on the cruciate ligaments, for example, which often causes them to tear. A good landing technique is the best way of avoiding this, but you can back this up with muscles that have been developed satisfactorily and above all 'intelligently'. You can achieve this by neuromuscular training and by runs with the maximum proprioceptive content. Various substrates are suitable for this – sand, gravel, grass etc. – and you can run on these even with eyes closed sometimes, to stimulate the perceptual capacity of the muscles, ligaments and joints. If there are dunes or mountains close by, then running up mountains is particularly to be recommended as an enhancement. Verstegen (2006: p. 185) recommends multi-storey car parks for training the 'energy system' in the city: the athlete should run up the ramps and walk back down the stairs. He doesn't need to do any endlessly long and above all tedious endurance runs, therefore, especially since these only cause stress to the body (Verstegen, 2006: p. 184: "Each time he puts a foot on the ground the stress is as great as seven times your body weight"). Instead of these, varied training stimuli are prescribed that address different systems: anaerobic and aerobic energy recovery should be practised in continuous alternation, with proprioceptive stimuli being integrated where possible. A training unit of this kind lasts 12 to 30 minutes. As the level of fitness improves, it's not the length of the runs that should be increased, as is observed in many cases, but the intensity.

Training stimuli in everyday situations

The recommended forms of training, which can be integrated into everyday situations, are also good for uniting coordinative and conditioning abilities. One of the best pieces of training equipment for improving balancing ability is the unicycle. Anyone who masters this can cover short distances on it and thus set a really good training stimulus. A skateboard can also render good service here. Practised handling on the skateboard develops balancing ability and has a positive effect on the feel for the board in kiting. These two training suggestions for improving coordinative ability can be expanded by further ideas, but training on unicycle or skateboard should suffice to make clear the underlying objective. The same goes for the following suggestions in other spheres.

Neuromuscular stimuli can also be incorporated into everyday living. There are many opportunities for using a wobble board even around the house; if you don't have one of these, there's something to be said for brushing your teeth or having a wash standing on one leg, for example. A journey on the underground may seem shorter and more interesting if you stand with one foot slightly raised off the floor, and if this isn't challenging enough, close your eyes as well and try to stay upright for as long as possible. It doesn't take a lot of imagination to discover a wealth of opportunities for proprioceptive training for kitesurfing as you go about your daily business.

If you would rather set a conditional stimulus, just as many opportunities present themselves. When you arrive at work on your bike, don't take the lift to your office, but use the stairs in a variety of ways for a spot of morning training. Step sequences and speeds can be varied satisfactorily to address different energy systems.

Conclusion: Continuous, varied and well coordinated training stimuli not only increase enjoyment and improve performance in kiting, but at the same time work as a prophylactic to injury and prevent damage as a result of over-stress.

10 Concluding comments

158

Kitesurfing is a terrific, versatile sport that brings us closer to the elements. It merits its designation as a sport. And sport calls for training – training that should in turn improve the athlete's sporting achievements and not least keep him healthy.

However, training processes are a long-term affair, requiring structure and thriving on continuity. This is especially true of extremely complex sports that make high demands on more than just a person's physique. To satisfy this profile of requirements for the sport of kitesurfing, which combines perceptual abilities and coordinative skills with a high level of physical fitness, it is advisable to create structured training processes and to set regular training goals. We have systematically shown the options for designing the training sessions efficiently, so that tricks are learnt faster, better and more reliably: a kitesurfing session begins ashore with a selection of training contents, which are then mentally rehearsed, so that following the warm-up and activation, effective training on the water is possible, which is challenging and enjoyable at the same time.

Regenerative activities following training on the water are just as important for long-term success and physical health as strengthening the relevant muscle groups and improving endurance.

Anyone who takes all the training tips given into account will not only be able to improve his performance, but will also feel more confident when kiting and will feel physically better afterwards. And that ultimately generates an even greater enjoyment of this terrific sport. We hope that the training concept outlined here contributes to this enjoyment, even if the question posed at the beginning – of what the surfing royalty of old Oceania would have said about our sport – must unfortunately remain unanswered.

GEAR TECHNOLOGY AND TIPS

The kite

It isn't our intention here by any means to try and resolve the much-debated question of which kite is best, especially since development could go in a different direction tomorrow. What is obvious is that kites have progressed rapidly in the last few years with regard to comfort and safety. Aerodynamics experts are constantly endeavouring to turn lateral forces into propulsion and 'lift', with some success. Think back to the kites of the last millennium, when kitesurfing was still observed quizzically or even marvelled at by beach-goers. Back then, kiters still struggled with fraying depower lines, or were swept unwillingly into the air by gusts. Fortunately, things are different now. Kites can be depowered very efficiently and cover a wide wind range, increasing not only ease of handling but also safety. And development is probably not yet at an end. Here we provide a brief summary of the types of kite that currently exist and the most important tips on kite use and care.

C-kites

C-kites have become very easy to operate over the years and increasingly more direct in their flying characteristics. However, they are not as commonly used any more. The oldest kites, the original two-liners, are scarcely ever seen nowadays and only surface very occasionally in kite schools or private ownership. C-kites with four lines are seen more frequently and are still produced by a few kite companies. They are distinguished by very direct flying behaviour, normally (depending on the aspect ratio) by strong power in the kiteloop and very high lateral forces. Most C-kites are now fitted with five lines. The fifth line on these kites is attached directly to the leading edge (by a line or V-line) and

leads through the *bar* to the chickenloop and safety system. Five-line kites can be relaunched extremely easily by simply pulling on the fifth line. They have a slightly less direct feeling and somewhat less power. The kite can also be depowered substantially by shortening the fifth line slightly. On five-line kites you should ensure in particular that the fifth line is not too short, as this would result in the kite kinking in the middle, which would have a negative effect on its flying characteristics. Five-liners also have a well-developed safety system, although this varies from manufacturer to manufacturer. Once triggered, the quick release can be reassembled in the water, enabling the kite to be relaunched relatively easily from the water.

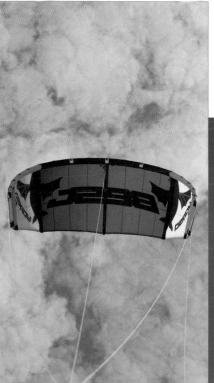

Bow kites

The latest and at present most widespread generation of bow kites increases riding comfort further: bow kites are equipped with *bridles*, and thanks to these, the lines are connected in such a way that the angle of attack of the kite can be changed far more than on C-kites, thus considerably increasing the ability to depower the kite. The application range is greatly increased by this method of connecting the lines, which is positively noticeable both when jumping and riding in the upper wind range. The projected surface is bigger in relation to the flat surface than on C-kites, offering the advantage that smaller kites can be flown. This not only increases safety, but a further considerable advantage is that riders don't need as many kites in their luggage. Bow kites make it easier to learn how to kitesurf, they make the sport safer and they're easy to fly. The safety systems are well developed too and for the most part can be reassembled in the water. Almost all bow kites on the market are fitted with four lines.

159

Hybrid kites

Many brands considered the switch from C-kite to bow kite as too extreme and developed an intermediate form, the hybrid kite. It is cut flatter than normal C-kites and most have round *tips*, having less area at the wing tips as a result. These are fitted not with *pullies* but with *bridles* in some cases. Hybrid kites come with four or five lines and in a variety of shapes. They are easier to depower than normal C-kites and have a wider application range. Compared with bow kites, hybrid kites represent an attempt to improve the handling characteristics.

Foil kites

Foil kites look like small paragliders and consist of air chambers which fill during flight or on launching. They are popular

for use as trainer kites and used increasingly in snow kiting, as they can be folded down to a very small size, don't have to be pumped up and can be launched easily on snow. They are only seen very infrequently on the water, and only a few companies manufacture this type of kite.

No recommendation can or should generally be made regarding a particular kite, especially as people always have their personal preferences and the important thing is to have fun with it. Every kiter has his own personal favourite to which he has become accustomed over time. When changing kites it often takes a long period of time to readjust, as different kites vary in respect of flying characteristics, lift and propulsion. To get as much enjoyment out of a kite as possible and to keep it in good condition for a long time, the following tips are worth noting:

Set-up: The lines must be adjusted to the kite. It's best if every kite has its own *bar*, so as to be able to adjust this to the kite in the optimum manner. When the kite is at the 12 o'clock position, the back lines shouldn't sag too much, as this would slow the kite down and even make large kites impossible to steer. Back lines that are too short also have a negative effect, as they would always be tensioned and over-sheet the trailing edge of the kite. The kite then tends to fall backwards, which is termed *back stall*. The optimum situation is when the back lines of the depowered kite (*bar* pushed away from body) sag slightly and pull can be felt on the back lines when the *bar* is powered (pulled in), but the kite should not fly backwards. If the depower system is fully powered (not pulled in), the kite can be additionally depowered if the wind increases by pulling the adjuster. The following generally applies: the set-up is good if a kite still flies well and can be controlled even when the rider is unhooked.

Pumping up the kite: Often kites are not pumped up sufficiently, due to fears that the tube might burst. Under-inflation has a negative effect on the kite's flying behaviour, because the less air there is in the front tube, the more a kite flexes in the air (*jellyfishing*). In a gusty wind in particular, the kite becomes very unsettled. We recommend that you pump the front tube up hard enough that it is difficult to compress it between the thumb and the index finger. If the *tube* can still be kinked easily just below the *tip*, it should be pumped up more.

Always check the pressure during and after pumping!

Repair: What's more annoying than to be standing on a beach somewhere ready to kite and discover that the kite has a tear in the fabric or a leak in a tube? And then to discover that no repair kit has been packed is surely no less irritating. If a repair kit is included, you need first to clean off any sand from the kite and dry it before attempting any kind of repair.

Repairing the tube: If a kite loses air in flight, the flying behaviour becomes very unsettled and the kite no longer reacts to steering movements. You should therefore check the kite briefly prior to launching in order to repair any damaged tube. Although this takes a little time, it isn't an especially complicated procedure:

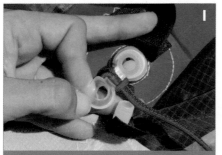

1

Take the plug out of the valve and attach a line (preferably a kite line) to it.

2

Open the sleeve at the rear end of the tube (normally only fixed by a Velcro fastener) and slowly withdraw the tube. The line will also be pulled through the sleeve.

3

Detach line and leave in sleeve and examine tube for the hole.

Tip: Often the tubes rip at the bottom end, so that is where you should check first. If the holes are too small to be seen immediately, the tube must be pumped up and submersed in water if necessary. Air bubbles should then appear at the point that needs repairing.

4

Roughen the area around the hole slightly using sandpaper (included in the repair kit supplied with the kite).

5

Then glue the repair patch (also included in the repair kit) onto the area in need of repair ...

6

... and press it down hard.

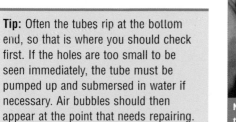

7

Now reattach the line in the sleeve to the tube valve.

9

To prevent the front end of the tube from twisting, the part ahead of the valve is simply turned inwards. It will then unfold when the tube is inflated later.

9

Fold the tube once, then pull it through smoothly and, with the valve on top (valve opening likewise on top), slowly with the aid of the line from the valve side. It is advisable when doing this for one person to pull the line through and another person to thread the tube in to ensure that it is pulled in straight.

10

The tube is pulled through more easily if the sleeve is placed flat.

On the beach it is advisable to clean sand off the board and use this as a solid base underneath the area requiring repair.

Pull the tube through until the valve is visible at the valve outlet hole. It is then pulled out carefully, the line removed and the valve cap reattached to the valve.

Using fresh water and a towel ...

Now the remaining end is folded in carefully on the other side ...

... first clean the area around the tear.

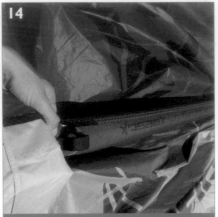

Now inflate the tube carefully and check that it isn't twisted or has been threaded in askew. It's quite important here to check whether the part between the front tube and the valve is filled correctly. If not, the threading must be repeated carefully.

162

Repairing the fabric: Unfortunately, torn fabric can also lead to an unpleasant kiting experience. Minuscule rips in the fabric caused, for example, by coral, can often cause the fabric to tear further. If you spot a small tear, it should be repaired immediately. Repair tape (spinnaker tape), obtainable from specialist shops, can be used not only to repair small rips fully but also to repair larger tears and so make the kite temporarily usable.

... and closed once more with the Velcro fastener.

Small holes like this one can cause large tears if the kite crashes into the water because once torn, the fabric can easily tear further under load.

While the area is drying, cut the spinnaker tape to size. Because the hole is repaired from both sides, two pieces of identical size are needed that should extend two to three centimetres beyond the tear. The corners of the tape are rounded to help it stick better.

Then cut the patch to size, and stick it onto the damaged area ...

... and press down hard. This is best done with your fingernail.

You then repeat this process on the other side of the fabric.

Repaired in this way, the kite can be used without a problem.

Board and fins

There are many different options when it comes to boards too. The question 'What is the best board?' is a highly individual one and the answer depends on a number of factors. Naturally the size and body weight of a kitesurfer generally play a not insignificant role in the choice of a board; time and again we see kiters between 1.85 and 1.90 metres tall trying to get a very narrow 1.22-metre board to plane, which can be pretty tricky – when it comes to going upwind, the owner of such a board will no longer be riding along happily! In the 1980s there was a time in windsurfing, too, when the shortness of the board appeared to indicate a radical approach on the part of the rider. But that phase quickly passed and the surfing world realized that other fundamental aspects were important. A similar situation exists in kitesurfing: to be able to cross waves in onshore wind, or to get back to where one started in the case of all other wind directions, going upwind has to be mastered, and although this is a question of technique, it can be helped along by suitable kit. Less experienced kitesurfers need a bigger board in any event, but even for advanced and expert kiters the following applies: to be able to go upwind, the board needs to be of a length that suits the size and weight of the rider. The width of the board should also be adequate, because wider boards start planing earlier and also make it easy to plane through wind lulls. Narrow boards are better for take-offs and jumping high than wide boards, which is noticeable when carving, for example. In addition to body measurements and riding skills, however, the kitesurfing style plays a key role. Anyone who prefers to use a smaller kite should ride a correspondingly larger, i.e. a longer and/or wider board, whereas a rider who flies his kite in the upper wind range needs a relatively small board. It goes without saying that riders who like wave-riding and spend a lot of time doing this without jumping should get themselves a wave-riding board. To satisfy all these passions and demands, there are various types of boards, which we'll introduce briefly.

Directional: The first kiteboards were directionals. In contrast to bidirectionals, they can only be ridden in one direction, thus only have fins at the rear of the board and offset footstraps. They are still used occasionally in kite schools or by kiters who like to combine high jumps with wave-riding. As it is not easy to ride in both directions with this board, it's necessary to turn around, which is very difficult, at least for beginners. This is the reason why directionals are no longer recommended for learning.

Twin tip: Twin tips come in all possible lengths and widths. Especially large models are used for kite school training and in extremely light wind conditions. Smaller sizes are suitable for freestyle riders. As already mentioned above, the size and width play a key role in relation to the style of kitesurfing for which they are used. Wider boards are particularly well suited to the wake style, as they make landing easier and enable a small kite to be flown. Narrower boards offer better edging than wide boards and have good take-off characteristics, which is of interest to all those who want to jump high. As we've already mentioned above, the size of the board is dependent on body weight and body size.

Surf-style board: These boards are very similar in shape to normal paddle surfboards. Many kiteboards for waves have been designed along the lines of the *tow-in* boards, and wave-riding is considerably easier on these boards. This is because the waves can be ridden more directly on account of the larger volume, which promotes a correspondingly good style. Smaller kites can even be used, which have a very positive effect in the waves. However, in this case the size of the board is also dependent on the size of

163

the wave, not only the rider. Larger boards are also ridden in especially big waves, but large surf-style boards are often used even in regions with light winds. These boards can be ridden with or without foot straps.

Skimboards: Skimboards are also gradually becoming more widespread in kiteboarding. Used originally for skimming across the water, these boards look a little like surfboards but are much smaller, more 'bellied' and without much volume. They are used in small waves or on shallow water and are ridden without foot straps.

Wakeskates: The wakeskate has been introduced from wakeboarding into kitesurfing. This type of board is ridden entirely without foot straps and mostly wearing strong sports shoes. Skate-

boarders in particular like these boards, because skateboard tricks are possible on the water too with these.

Fins: The size of the fins also has an influence on the upwind abilities of the board, the larger the fins, the more strongly they hold and the better they can counter drift and thus positively assist in going upwind. Nevertheless, when choosing fins, take into account that smaller fins make the board loose in the sense of easy to turn, which is helpful in manoeuvres such as board switching. Riders who prefer to perform their manoeuvres in the wakeboard style prefer using small fins. Ultimately, though, it's a question of personal choice: some riders want to turn fast and jump high, others want to ride waves, and then there are those who just want to cruise a little. So it is understandable that a

difference of a centimetre in fin length can produce considerable differences with regard to board use and makes sense of the following comment by board developer Tad Ciastula: "Some guys are riding 6, because they like to pop off the fins", meaning that some riders use bigger fins so that they can build up greater pressure on take-off, which in turn gives them longer airtime.

The *bar*

Generally the best idea is to buy the *bar* that goes with the kite. On most *bars* the lines are then already adjusted correctly. There are special 4-liner, 5-liner and bow kite *bars* to match the kites. The *bars* can be fitted with lines in a range of lengths: the usual length is between 15 and 28 metres. Long lines make a kite slower, short lines reduce the power of the kite slightly (except in kiteloops). For normal kiting, lines of 23 to 26 metres long should be used.

To make your *bar* and lines last longer, it's advisable to rinse them off regularly in fresh water and to ensure that the lines are always wound properly. Winding in a 'figure of 8' and fixing the lines on the *bar* ends with a half hitch will effectively prevent 'line tangles'.

Kristin's and Marc's boards are specially tailored to their requirements. Kristin rides boards that are designed for competition conditions and wakeboard tricks. Marc's boards are designed for radical turns in the waves.

The harness

Unlike windsurfing, kitesurfing isn't possible without a harness, even if *unhooked* jumps make it appear so. Without the harness, the kitesurfing session would only last a few minutes, even for highly trained athletes, on account of the high forces that the kite generates. Two types of harness can be distinguished: beginners spend a relatively large amount of time with their kite in the 12 o'clock position, in order to orient their board for the launch, for example. For them a seat harness is more comfortable, as it cannot slip in spite of the upward pull. But even advanced riders, who prefer to counteract the pull of the kite by means of a somewhat more comfortable 'sitting' posture, can revert to seat harnesses if the reduced freedom of movement isn't a problem for them. The waist harness offers greater freedom of movement. When buying a harness of this type, however, you should take care to ensure that it fits well, as in high positions of the kite in particular it has a tendency to ride upwards, causing uncomfortable pressure on the lower ribs.

Secure lines with a half hitch!

Kristin Boese took up kitesurfing at the beginning of 2002. She began competing in German and international competitions in the same year and has already been crowned world champion seven times and has been competing in five different disciplines. The support she now receives from her sponsors Best Kiteboarding, LTU, RIAL, Maui Magic and Anton Kiteboards enables her to compete full-time as a professional kitesurfer.

Marc Ramseier is one of the top waveriders. As a true master in this field, he shows us skilful wave-riding in this book. For a long time Marc was a Freestyle World Cup kiter and regularly featured among the top ten. Now, however, he concentrates on his true passion and is a professional wave-rider. He is sponsored by Gin Kites, Da Kine, CP Eyewear and Quatro Surfboards.

Christian Spreckels has a master's degree in sport science. He is an assistant lecturer at the University of Hamburg and also coaches in various sports. He has been surfing for 22 years and has been an enthusiastic kitesurfer for the last six years.

Alterman, D. & Stoll, O., *Sportpsychologie. Ein Lehrbuch in 12 Lektionen*. Aachen, 2005.
(Sports psychology. A textbook in 12 lessons.)

Bierhoff, D. & Alterman, N., *Sportpsychologie*. Stuttgart, 1986.
(Sports psychology.)

Buchbauer, J., *Präventives Muskeltraining zur Behebung von Haltungsfehlern*, 2nd edition. Schorndorf, 2001.
(Preventive training to rectify posture faults.)

Csikszentmihalyi, M., *Das flow-Erlebnis. Jenseits von Angst und Langeweile: Im Tun aufgehen*, 7th edition. Stuttgart, 1999.
(Beyond boredom and anxiety. Experiencing flow in work and play.)

Daugs, R., Einige Bemerkungen zum Beitrag von Horst Tiwald 'Zur Theorie des Mentalen Trainings'. In: *Leibesübungen - Leibserziehung*, Vol. 26(9), 1972, pp. 194–195.
(Some comments on the article by Horst Tiwald 'On the theory of mental imaging'.)

Eberspächer, H., *Mentale Trainingsformen in der Praxis*. Oberhaching, 1990.
(Mental imaging forms in practice.)

Fetz, F., Mentale Trainingsmethoden. In: *Praxis der Leibesübungen*, 14, 1973, pp. 51–56.
(Mental imaging methods.)

Fodor, J.A., *The Modularity of Mind*. Cambridge, Mass., 1983.

Gabler, W.H., Hauser, O.H., Hug, H.O. & Steiner, H. (Hg.), *Psychologische Beratung und Diagnostik im Leistungssport*. Frankfurt, 1985.
(Psychological consultancy and diagnostics in performance sport.)

Geiger, U. & Schmid, C., *Muskeltraining mit dem Thera-Band*. Munich, 2004.
(Muscle training using the Thera-Band.)

Groos, K., *The Play of Man*. New York, 1901.

Hebbel-Seeger, A., *Snowboarding. Guide to Ride*. Aachen, 2001.

Hossner, E.-J., Beim Fertigkeitslernen im Sport: Keine Angst vor Überforderungen! In: *Sportspsychologie*, Vol. 7(2), 1993, pp. 17–20.
(Learning skills in sport: No fear of being overchallenged!)

Kröger, G., *Wellenreiten. Ein ethnologischer Beitrag zur Geschichte des Wellenreitens. Hausarbeit zur Erlangung des Magistergrades*. Institut für Völkerkunder, Göttingen, 1979.
(Surfing. An ethnological contribution on the history of surfing. Thesis to gain a Master's Degree.)

Leist, K.-H., Transfer beim Erwerb von Bewegungskönnen. In: *Sportwissenschaft*, Vol. 4(2), 1974, pp. 136–163.
(Transfer in the acquisition of movement prowess.)

Leist, K.-H., *Lernfeld Sport*. Cologne, 1993.
(Sport as a development field.)

Michaelis, P., *Moderne Funktionelle Gymnastik*. Aachen, 2000.
(Modern functional gymnastics.)

Nagel, C.V. & Spreckels, C., *Mit Ballspielen zum Tennis*. Aachen, 2003.
(Through ball games to tennis.)

Nickel, C., Zernial, V.O., Musahl, U.V., Hansen, P.U., Zantop, P. & Petersen, W., Prospective study of kitesurfing injuries. In: *J Sports Med.*, Vol. 32(4), 2004, pp. 921–927.

Overschmidt, R.H. & Gliewe, R., *Sportbootführerschein Binnen*. Bielefeld, 2004.
(Recreational craft licence for inland waterways.)

Petersen, W., Hansen, U., Zernial, O. et al., Mechanism and prevention of kitesurfing injuries (in German). In: *Sportverletzung-Sportschaden*, Vol. 16, 2002, pp. 115–121.

Petersen, W., Zantop, T., Steensen, M., Hypa A.T., Wessolowski, T. & Hassenpflug, J., Prävention von Verletzungen der unteren Extremität im Handball: Erste Ergebnisse des Kieler Handball-Verletzungs-Präventionsprogrammes. In: *Sportverletzung-Sportschaden*, Vol. 16(3), 2002, pp. 122–126.
(Prevention of lower limb injuries in handball: Initial results of the Kiel Handball Injury Prevention Programme.)

Syer, J. & Connolly, C., *Sporting Body, Sporting Mind: Athlete's Guide to Mental Training*. Cambridge, 1984.

Syer, J. & Connolly, C., *Psychotraining für Sportler*. Reinbek, 1987.
(Psychotraining for athletes.)

Tiwald, H., 'Mentales Training'. Erwiderung auf die Kritik von Daugs. In: *Leibesübungen - Leiberserziehung*, 26 Jg., 1972, Heft 9, p. 196. ('Mental imaging'. A reply to the criticism by Daugs.)

Tiwald, H., Zur Theorie des Mentalen Trainings. In: *Leibesübungen - Leiberserziehung*, 26 Jg., 1972, Heft 5, pp. 98–102. (On the theory of mental imaging.)

Tiwald, H., Mentales Training und sportliche Leistungsfähigkeit In: *Leibesübungen - Leiberserziehung*, Vol. 27(3), 1973, pp. 56–60. (Mental imaging and athletic performance.)

Verstegen, M. & Williams, P., *Core Performance*. Munich, 2006.

Volpert, W., *Optimierung von Trainingsprogrammen; Untersuchungen über den Einsatz des mentalen Trainings beim Erwerb sensomotorischer Fertigkeit*, 2nd edition. Lollar/Lahn, 1976. (Optimizing training programmes: Studies on the use of mental imaging in the acquisition of sensomotory skills.)

Wiemann, K., Untersuchungen zum mentalen Training turnerischer Bewegungsabläufe. In: *Die Leibeserziehung*, Vol. 20(2), 1971, pp. 36–41. (Studies on the mental imaging of gymnastic movement sequences.)

Ziegler, M., Kwiatowsky, A., Reer, R. & Braumann, K.M., Verletzungen beim Kitesurfen, Ursachen & Präventionsmöglichkeiten. In: *Deutsche Zeitschrift für Sportsmedizin*, 56(7/8), 2005, p. 256. (Injuries in kitesurfing, causes and options for prevention.)

Special thanks

Special thanks go to Marc, for his kind support and constant willingness to help; to Karo and Tom for their terrific support and the many hours of free Internet use; to Club Mistral/Skyriders for their kind assistance; to Robbin and Katrin of the Kitebeach Hotel in Cabarete for a wonderful time and the special deals; to Victor Martins and Eduardo Urdanetta of Margaritakitesurf.com for making the trip possible and, of course, to our families and friends.

Kristin Boese

An affectionate thank-you goes to my small daughter Johanna, who at the tender age of 11 weeks had to put up all too often with her Daddy sitting at his desk; to my partner Claudia, who showed great understanding on the whole; to Maike Lundt of Werbesalon, who kindly put together the graphics; to Frieder Bachteler and Hauke Bischoff for the critical corrections; to Marc Ziegler of the Sports Medicine Department of the University of Hamburg; Dirk Jahnke of the Wassersportschule Rostock and Knut Peyer of the Segelschule Prüsse for their technical advice. I would also like to give special thanks here to Kristin for her dependable and genial cooperation.

Christian Spreckels

167

Photographs:
Marc Ramseier
Christian Black
Roberto Foresti
Ian Trafford
Steven Whitesell
Alexey Kashin
Gavin Buttler

Graphics:
Werbesalon, Hamburg.